Power of Purpose

*MY JOURNEY OF FINDING
MY SUPERPOWERS, WHILE
NAVIGATING THROUGH PAIN*

Shermie Hargrove

13TH & JOAN

For permission requests, write to the publisher, addressed "Attention: Permissions Coordinator," 205 N. Michigan Avenue, Suite #810, Chicago, IL 60601. 13th & Joan books may be purchased for educational, business or sales promotional use. For information, please email the Sales Department at sales@13thandjoan.com.

Printed in the U. S. A.

First Printing, November 2024.

Library of Congress Cataloging-in-Publication Data has been applied for.

Paperback ISBN: 978-1-961863-94-1
Hardcover ISBN: 978-1-961863-93-4

To my incredible sister circle, especially my "Eight" who have stood by me and contributed to my purpose journey. Your unwavering support and love have been my foundation.

To those in my circle, those who stood in my corner, and those I have yet to meet—thank you for loving me through the past, present, and future. I am truly blessed with the best. This journey is ours.

To my forever Ace—Lashaundra Stansel, may your soul continue to rest. Thank you for guarding me and I miss you!

Contents

Preface

*Y*ou have to go through some adversity, pain, and trauma to get your super-powers. Nothing you are going through is unintentional. While you will be tempted to find the good in every difficult situation, the goal is to gain a deeper understanding and learn more about who you are so that your purpose becomes clear.

Once you realize how powerful it is to survive all that comes your way in life, you will understand what your purpose is. We all must make an effort to understand the power of our purpose. The challenge is to open ourselves up to the pain so that we are able to birth a new light.

Introduction

My Story, My Glory

We must become bigger than we have ever been.
SHERMIE HARGROVE

art survivor. Part warrior. All woman. That's who I am, and this is my story.

I believe we all enter this world with a to-do list from God—endure suffering, be kind to others, overcome obstacles, etc. Each task is uniquely personal to each individual, and through our life's journey, we gradually come to understand our purpose. As we grow in age, we should also grow in wisdom and character. The challenges we face along the way are the building blocks that contribute to the foundation of what we build throughout our lifetime. As we continue to grow and evolve, we start to realize that every win, every loss, every joy, and every pain was meant to happen just the way He planned it.

For me, this journey has led to the revelation that my purpose is to give back, to help others find their way, particularly young women who are searching for their own purpose. I believe that God has allowed me to experience certain trials so that I can relate to others who face similar struggles. My purpose is to share my story, and that is why I am writing this book. I've come to understand that my experiences, both good and bad, have equipped me to be a blessing to others, to guide them, and to inspire them to embrace their own authenticity and purpose.

My life has been marked by overcoming significant loss: The loss of my mother, brother, grandmother, and father–in that order. I've faced homelessness, dealt with a parent's addiction, survived molestation, endured heartbreak, and navigated the challenges of being a single mother. These experiences, as painful as they were, have shaped me into who I am today. As enlightened as I may sound now, it was only as I approached my 40s that I truly began to understand my purpose. I stopped asking, "Why me?" and instead started asking, "What can I learn from this experience?"

Connecting the dots of my life, I realized that my pain was not in vain. It was leading me to my purpose. Everything I went through was preparing me to help others, to tell my story, and to be a mentor. I've come to see that my wounds, once healed, have become a source of strength not only for myself but for others.

In everything I do, I try to see the good in people. I believe this is a gift from God, though it can sometimes feel like both a blessing and a curse. I have a deep sense of compassion and grace for others because I can see their souls and understand their struggles. It doesn't matter if they are family, friends, or strangers. This understanding sometimes leads me to justify behaviors because I know how hard it can be to overcome certain challenges. You will read stories about how this compassion has hurt me in the past. Although I may still be vulnerable to it, I am no longer a victim of it. I am cognizant of my overt concern for others in a way that no longer hurts me. My heart continues to go out to those who have suffered, especially those who didn't ask for the pain they've endured.

Today, I am a mother to a 23-year-old son whom I am raising to be a positive contributor to society. I have started a nonprofit organization to help young girls ages 11-16 build a strong foundation—spiritual, mental, and physical. In my career, which has involved a lot of recruiting, I've taken individuals under my wing, helping them soar in their careers by coaching them and matching the highest quality candidates with mid-sized companies from a myriad of industries in search of the best talent available. Though the Hargrove family is small, I see myself as its leader, guiding my nieces and nephews to understand who we are and what we stand for by providing job opportunities within my business.

When people tell me how I've touched their lives, how I've impacted them, or when they show up for me, it reaffirms my belief that I am living out my purpose. My story is my glory, and I speak from a place of experience. Despite the flaws of the people I've known, I can always find something good to say about them.

Throughout this book, I will share stories of the people who have shaped my life. My father, despite his drug problem, was a giver and a man of peace. I don't recall ever seeing him upset. Now there were stories about how he wasn't the kind of guy you wanted to mess with, but I never saw that side of him. Instead, he came across as an intellectual. His mind processed numbers like a calculator and his memory was better than a Jeopardy contestant's.

Then there was my grandmother, who had a reputation of being strong and fiery, but shocked people with her modesty when they would praise her for a display of kindness when it mattered most. The greatest influencer of all may have been my brother. He was loyal to the family and looked out for all of us, even the adults. He was so driven at a young age that he unfortunately completed God's to-do list early, and there was nothing left for him to do here. Finally. there's Aunt Roz. She was a cancer survivor and a fighter. The woman didn't understand the word quit. She would become the person I modeled myself after. These people, along with the challenges I've faced, have all contributed to my understanding of purpose.

Ultimately, I believe that purpose is birthed through pain. When we endure painful experiences, we have the opportunity to learn, to grow, and to serve others. God doesn't put us through pain to see us suffer. He does it to make us better, to equip us to share our testimony with others. My story is one of victory. I hope that through this book, I can help others find their own victory in the midst of their pain. This is my purpose, and this is why I am sharing it with you.

1

Where Legacy Began

Grandmothers are a hint of magic and a dash of love.
SHERMIE HARGROVE

When I was growing up, Tuscaloosa, Alabama was a sanctuary for me. A small Southern town smack dab in the middle of the state, it was the type of place where everyone knew their neighbors. When you walked down the street, every person on their porch waved at you and said hello. Anybody who was raised in that town could easily point out which house belonged to the Johnsons, the Merriweathers, or the Simpsons.

Tuscaloosa was a small town, but it wasn't a one-traffic-light stop on Highway 82 either. There was a train station and an airport. In fact, it was the state capital before Montgomery. The original capitol building still stands, giving the community a historic feel. It was home to majestic magnolia trees, a spectacular riverfront, and American Gothic-style houses. It was also the home of our family's matriarch, my grandmother Leatha. She was a little lady with a big heart. If shelter and protection were a person, it would be her.

She cared for me and my brother from as early as I can remember. She was the extension of the love that I had received from my own mother before she passed away when I was only three years old. My mother was grandma's only girl. That's probably why grandma named her Queen. She may have been the middle child, but she was never ignored. Her older and younger brothers kept her upright like bookends. Once my mother passed away, all of grandma's love for her needed somewhere to go and it ended up raining down on me like a quiet storm. Although I technically didn't live with my grandmother, I spent a lot of summers, spring breaks, and holidays with her in Tuscaloosa.

Sadly, I don't have many memories of my mother, however, a piece of her definitely lives within me. Wherever I'd go with my grandmother—church, the grocery store, the gas station, anywhere—someone would always come up to me and tell me how much I reminded them of my mother. I found that it was commonplace to get that kind of reaction in a small town where everyone knew each other. In my own hometown of Atlanta, I was anonymous. They call it the city too busy to hate, but it is also the city too busy for you to get to know your neighbor. In Tuscaloosa, I was Queenie's girl, and I felt a little like a queen myself anytime someone recognized my mother in me. The smiles I received warmed me up on the inside and in my head, I heard them calling me Your Grace. The interactions reassured me that my mother had made some kind of impact or impression on people in the short amount of time she was here.

I pictured her running around town in pigtails and frilly dresses with patent leather shoes and those fancy ankle socks. I could hear her voice saying, "Yes sir" and "Yes ma'am" to all the people in the neighborhood as was expected of a young girl growing up in the South. Atlanta was technically still in the South, but it didn't have that same Southern charm, probably because of the influx of northerners who decided to move south once Atlanta started getting popular. Sometimes I wondered why my mother ever left Tuscaloosa. Although she had passed away years earlier, I could still see the gleam in my grandmother's eyes whenever someone mentioned my mother's name. There was, however, a downside to constantly bringing up my mother's memory.

On occasion, I'd look out the window when granny came home from running errands. She'd take a moment to stop sobbing and gather herself before coming inside, wiping away her tears. Behind closed doors, sometimes joyful memories turned into painful reminders. Grandma used to cry so much. I can still see her in her room as I peeked through her partially opened door. She would sit on the edge of the bed, thinking no one was watching. I would hear her sobbing and see her shoulders convulsing as she let air out of her lungs. I would retreat from the sight. I was too young and afraid to confront her and possibly console her. Instead, I would see her half an hour later, coming out of her room with eyes still red and puffy from crying. Had I been old enough to process everything that happened, I would have asked my grandmother more about my mother just to hear my mother's story in my grandmother's voice. Unfortunately, I never got that chance.

For a time, we were up in grandma's house like three the hard way. And what a time was had! It was me, grandma, and my brother Jarvis, who was five years older than me. We spent more time getting on each other's nerves than playing together still, I learned a lot from him. I fondly remember walking with him to the Piggly Wiggly where he would sometimes buy me a sour pickle. When grandma was with us, I remember how she would point and pick out which pickled pig feet she wanted from a big, glass jar. My favorite thing to get was soda pop because we'd get a nickel for every bottle we brought back to the store to recycle. Grandma would let me and my brother keep the change we received back and buy candy with it. Now and Later and Jolly Ranchers might have been my favorites.

When we'd get back to grandma's house from running errands, usually in the evening, it was normal to hear a knock on her screen door from a neighbor: "Hey Ms. Leatha. I got your rent!" As I got a little older, I realized that my grandmother was a boss and everyone treated her like one. She owned a couple of small apartment buildings that were near her house. Tenants would come weekly to get ahead on their rent because they knew that Ms. Leatha don't play! If they could look into the house through the screen window and see the television in the background, they were welcome to drop by. If that front door was closed and that porch light was off, you had better respect her boundaries. While grandma had this sandpaper exterior, she had a paper mache around her heart. The tenants who stopped by the house to pay their rent were the same tenants my grandmother had extended grace to in the past when they didn't have all the money for rent.

Those apartments provided a steady cash flow for grandma and a steady flow of friends for me. That's where most of the neighborhood kids lived, and they became my playmates. Once their parents found out I was Ms. Leatha's granddaughter, I don't think those kids had a choice but to be nice to me. It's likely they were told they had to play with me. We indulged in all the childhood games that were popular at the time–hide and seek; red light, green light; hot peas and butter, you name it. Nevertheless, a bunch of adventurous kids could still get bored on a hot summer day and end up looking for trouble.

"Shermie, get your behind down here right now!'" my grandmother yelled up to me from the street when she caught me playing on an apartment rooftop with some other kids acting like gravity didn't exist. "Get from up there before you break your neck!"

"I'm sorry, grandma. We weren't going to jump. I'm coming down," I yelled back to her. While it's true I wasn't going to jump off the two-story building, some of the boys talked about doing it. They thought if they landed in the grass, they wouldn't get hurt. I was too scared to consider it. I thought about Peter Pan and Wendy floating around in Neverland, but I didn't believe I could fly. And there was one boy I wouldn't even stand too close to. He played too much and I believed he might push me or one of the other girls off the roof because he liked us. Boys at that age were so weird. Grandma might have actually saved my life but she turned from hero to villain as she made me pick out the switch she used to beat me after that. I had previously learned to pick the oldest and driest branch I could find, hoping it would be brittle enough to break after a few good whacks. Although I was the one getting punished, anytime grandma punished me, it seemed like it hurt her more.

At least one year, my summer with grandma was extended into the school year. I still have the professional school photos of me she bought from Sears or JC Penneys. I had on a yellow dress against a black background with a double-exposure silhouette of my side profile. It was the latest photo technology at the time. Every morning, I'd get dressed for school and rush to the kitchen to help make pancakes from scratch, the only way to make them if you're from the South, she would boast.

It wasn't just a life of leisure for me at grandma's house. I learned a lot by her side. After school, I'd help her tend to her garden. She showed me how to shuck corn, and I remember snapping peas until my fingers were tender. The only solace I had from the numbing of my thumbs was that my brother was not spared from my grandmother's to-do list. She didn't view this as a woman's work. It was more like, "You wanna eat too, don't you?" Whether he'd excuse himself to play video games or go bike riding with his friends, the second he entered back into the house he'd be grabbed by the ear to sit beside me on the floor before that rickety, old screen door could even click shut.

To make the best of it, my brother and I made a game out of who could snap the most, the fastest, which ended up in a mess of pea pods on the floor that did not please grandma. Not only did she make us sweep up the mess, we had to mop every inch of the wooden floorboards before her tea kettle flipped its lid and whistled like a train pulling into its station. Our next competition was competing to see who could dry the floors the fastest before grandma finished her tea and came back inside from the front porch. It wasn't too bad though because my brother would play some rap music on his cassette player while we did our work.

The most egregious of our civil duties came in the form of pulling weeds in grandma's garden. My chores were mainly confined to the household, proba-bly due to my age, but my brother's chores were typically located outside and required more physical labor. After assisting my grandmother with making pancakes every morning, I was given the order to fetch my brother for break-fast. I found him outside hunched over a mound of plucked weeds with roots and dirt hanging from the ends of each batch. When he spotted me, he told me to come over and pull some for myself. It took a while for me to get the hang of it. I'd bend over and pull but only managed to come up with a handful of stems, no roots in sight.

"No, Shermie," he would say. "You gotta get the root, otherwise the weeds will continue to grow and come back. They ain't gone just 'cuz you can't see them anymore. You gotta dig down to where it all began. That's how you get rid of them." I would reflect on his words later on in life, not knowing he was giving advice that extended beyond the task at hand. Jarvis was always wise beyond his years.

All the chores and hard work was worth it because at the end of the summer, I got to celebrate my birthday with grandma. I was born in August, so I would

"No, Shermie," he would say. "You gotta get the root, otherwise the weeds will continue to grow and come back. They ain't gone just 'cuz you can't see them anymore. You gotta dig down to where it all began. That's how you get rid of them." I would reflect on his words later on in life, not knowing he was giving advice that extended beyond the task at hand. Jarvis was always wise beyond his years.

still be on summer break when it rolled around. She would go into her stash for me. Her bank was underneath floorboards in her bedroom, not the ones we had to mop in the living room. She would put a little cash away for me and my brother until we got there each summer. I got a kick out of watching the whole process. She'd slide her bed to the side with her hip, then move a rug she had covering the floor. It reminded me of the same motion she would make when she pulled our blankets back for us to climb into bed. Like a ballerina, grandma would gently tap on the floorboards with her toe until she heard the right sound, a distinct creak. Then she would pull up a floorboard and go into her stash. There might not have been any gold coins underneath her floor, but she would give me cash and would always buy me something too. The birthday celebration was never over until she made me a coconut cake. It was a moist, white cake with buttercream frosting and coconut flakes sprinkled all over it like fresh, fallen snow. A big slice of that coconut cake and a scoop of vanilla bean ice cream was all I needed to eat on my birthday. It was better than any other meal I could think of.

Another highlight from my summers in Tuscaloosa was seeing my grandfather pull up on me and my brother. He drove a big, black Cadillac, and that thing was always clean. His hood ornament gleamed coming down the street looking like the North Star. We used to ride around in that car like we were in a parade, waving at people out the window while granddad gently tapped his horn whenever we drove past someone he recognized in the old neighborhood. He seemed to always have a cassette tape playing while he was riding. The music was never too loud, just loud enough to hear him coming if you weren't deep in a conversation with someone else. He loved listening to Al Green and Marvin Gaye. Although he and grandma separated a long time ago, I appreciated the relationship they still shared. They were still cordial. Grandma would still fix a plate for him whenever he stopped by, collard greens included. I wondered if grandma always made greens just in case he stopped by. Sometimes he would come inside and have long conversations with grandma.

That didn't mean that granny didn't have anybody. Her special friend was like a step-grandfather to us. They never married, but he came around a lot. I remember seeing him get on the floor, sitting between grandma's legs getting his scalp greased with Royal Crown Hairdressing. I watched grandma part his hair, creating sections to moisturize his scalp. You could tell there was a special connection between them. He'd still be there by the time Jarvis and I went to bed, but he was never there in the morning when we woke up.

I look back at those times with such fond memories. The love my grandmother gave me and Jarvis was insurmountable. Grandma represented stability for me and my brother. We didn't really get that with our father. She filled a void with the untimely passing of our mother. Grandma was my refuge and my respite. She was my protector. Grandma's house was my sanctuary from a world of turbulence. Eventually, I learned that the world was much bigger than grandma's reach. Despite her fierce reputation and the admiration of the community, she couldn't be everywhere all the time. As I got a little older and grew beyond the radius of her safety zone, new memories were created, ones that still haunt me now.

PURPOSE NOTE

My purpose in sharing this part of my journey is to honor the strength I inherited from my grandmother, a woman who faced life's hardships with quiet resilience. Her presence was a steady force in my life, even though she rarely showed affection. I can't recall her smile or laugh, nor did I witness her lean on anyone for help—even though her special friend was around. She carried everything on her shoulders. While I now wonder if I ever truly saw her happy, I understand that her light still shone in how she cared for us, providing stability amidst her grief and pain. The echoes of her life shaped the foundation of my strength. As you continue reading, you'll see how this strength, even in silence, connects to the other women who raised me.

2

Boundaries Misunderstood

Beware of lions pretending to be lambs.
SHERMIE HARGROVE

When I was still a kid, the film *The Color Purple* came out. It was the screen adaptation of a book by Alice Walker. I don't think I saw the movie when it first came out, but I do remember watching it with my grandmother at some point. I remember the movie being very controversial at the time. A lot of Black folks didn't like how Black men were depicted. Of course, I was too young to process anything the adults were talking about. *The Color Purple* was turned into a Broadway musical when I was an adult, prompting me to revisit the original movie. I wanted to familiarize myself with the film again before I heard Fantasia Barrino turn repressing dialogue into an enchanting song. After watching the movie from a grown woman's perspective with plenty of experience in the world, there was a quote in the movie that stood out to me. Sofia, the character played by Oprah Winfrey, said, "A girl child ain't safe in a family of men."

Hearing her say that out loud was like a hypnotist counting backward from 10. It took me to my sunken place as I experienced dissociative amnesia. I had blocked out a lot of the trauma I went through in my younger years to protect myself from the damage I had experienced as a young girl. I came to accept the harsh realization that I had been molested as a child. It wasn't a dream. It wasn't even a nightmare. It was a real-life event, and it happened to me.

I called him Uncle Lester, but he wasn't my blood uncle. We were related but I'm not sure exactly how. I think he was my uncle's son but because of the age difference between us, I called him uncle out of respect. Come to find out he didn't deserve any respect from me. This man violated me in my grandmother's house! The more I think about it, the more enraged I get. I wasn't the only object of his evil. He molested my stepsister as well. My father had remarried by that time. My stepmother was an entrepreneur, but she was also my father's side piece when my mother was still alive. Her daughter, Shannon, had to be at least 10 years older than I was.

Of course, my grandmother wasn't home when the abuse occurred. Had she been there, she would have protected me and nothing would have happened. But grandma couldn't be there all the time. She may have been running errands or visiting my mother's grave. She did that a lot. She'd always take flowers and clean off her grave. Uncle Lester had a reputation for drinking too much, which is why grandma would never let him stay too long. When he got too many spirits inside of him, his demons came out. On this particular day, Uncle Lester stopped by the house while grandma was gone. This was the first time he was in the house alone with me and my stepsister that I could remember. Unfortunately, one time was all he needed.

He started with Shannon. I could hear her in the bedroom arguing with him, but I didn't know why. All of a sudden, there was this big commotion and I heard a loud thud. Then I heard Shannon yell, "Get the fuck off of me!" She screamed it at the top of her lungs. It startled me. I think she was loud enough for the neighbors to hear, but no one came to our rescue. Next, I heard a door slam, and a few seconds later I saw Uncle Lester standing at my bedroom door, rubbing the back of his head. I imagine Shannon somehow got the best of him and he gave up. He had that lustful look in his eye like he would not be denied. He just needed some easier prey, so he came to me instead.

Initially, I liked Uncle Lester. He was really funny and always made me laugh. Other people must have felt the same way because everyone would smile when he walked into a room. "Hey Lester" would echo through the house at family gatherings. I didn't understand why grandma would make him leave when he had too much to drink. She could have just let him stay at her house and sleep it off, but I was about to find out why she didn't want him around. "My, my, Shermie. What you in here doing?" His words were slurred and he stumbled when he stepped but when he smiled, his teeth were still as white and straight as lines on a highway. That was a part of his appeal.

"Nothing. Just playing with my toys," I answered.

"Yeah? Can I play with you?" Uncle Lester asked. He didn't wait for an answer. He sat down on the bed with me and grabbed one of my dolls. "Oh. This one here is really pretty. What's her name?"

"Barbie," I responded. I hadn't taken the time to name her myself.

"Well look here, Barbie. I really like those nice, long legs of yours," he said as he hiked up the dress I had on the doll. "But you know what, Shermie? Barbie ain't got nothing on you. I can already tell you're gonna be tall, dark, and lovely, with legs for days!"

That's when Uncle Lester reached out and touched my leg. His actions left me frozen. I stopped combing my other doll's hair and was paralyzed. I didn't know for sure what was about to happen, but my intuition told me it wasn't anything good. I second-guessed my feelings because Uncle Lester was family. He wouldn't do anything to harm me. I knew something just went down in Shannon's room, but that was different. Shannon wasn't his blood. That was my stepsister. He wouldn't try the same thing with me. Lester stared at me with black, beady eyes. There was nothing behind them, like a reptile's. Then he stood up, like he snapped out of his trance.

"Girl, what you getting all nervous about? Keep on playing," he said and flashed his perfect teeth again. He headed for the door and I was relieved. He wasn't going to bother me. Or at least that's what I thought. Lester got to the bedroom door and stopped. He grabbed the door handle and closed the door from the inside. I heard the knob lock click, and then he turned back around toward me.

"I know a little game that we can play together," he said in a voice at least two octaves lower than usual. He came back over toward me and sat back down on my bed. "We're gonna play the Tickle Game. I'm gonna touch you in certain places and you're going to tell me if it tickles."

I nodded my head in agreement because I didn't think I had a choice. He started by taking off his shoes and sitting Indian-style on the bed facing me. Next he grabbed my leg and set it in his lap. He proceeded to take off my sock. He rubbed the top of my foot. I remember how smooth and soft his hand felt. Then he tickled the bottom of my foot and I pulled away and laughed a little bit, not because I was having fun but because it was a natural reaction.

"Okay! One point for me," he said joyfully. "Now it's your turn, but I'm going to help you out." My foot was still in his lap. He pulled it closer until it touched his crotch. Then he rubbed my foot back and forth against it until I could feel a bulge in his pants stiffen and grow.

"Ahhhh. That don't tickle, but it sure feels good!" He rejoiced. "You're doing a great job, Shermie. You are a special girl, and we're gonna be SPECIAL friends. All the boys are gonna be chasing after you when you get older. You're so pretty, and you've got a great body. I wanna show you what to expect when a boy shows interest in you. But there's a catch. You can't tell anybody about what I'm going to show you. I'm breaking the man code by telling you this. Guys would be mad if they knew I showed you all our tricks. And this is something your grandma can't show you. She don't know nothing about this, and we gotta keep it that way. You understand?"

I was so naive at the time. I had blocked so much of this out that it's hard for me to place it on my timeline, but I think I had to be about 8 or 9 years old when this took place. I was old enough to know that I liked boys, and I thought Lester was handsome. I did like him complimenting me. Still, I didn't want him touching me, but I didn't know what to do to make him stop.

"Yes. I understand, Uncle Lester."

"See? Good girl! I knew I could trust you," Lester said as if he bet on the right horse at the racetrack. "Now let's get back to our game!"

This time he sat behind me and reached under my arms. I clenched my arms tight against my side because I was ticklish there, but I didn't laugh. The next thing I knew, I felt Uncle Lester's lips touch the back of my neck. I scrunched up my shoulders to get him off of me but he wouldn't stop. I wasn't like Shannon. I had no idea how to fight off a grown man. Instead, I let him do whatever it was he was trying to do. His hand moved from my underarms to the front of my chest. I barely had breasts at the time, but Lester began rubbing my chest regardless.

"Does that feel good to you?" Lester asked.

I shrugged my shoulders because I really didn't know. He asked me to stand up. I did what I was told.

"Now model for me. Turn all the way around. And do it slowly."

I had on a one piece dress, possibly a school uniform. I turned around in a circle and curtsied at the end.

"Bravo Shermie! Bravo."

At this point, Lester reached out to me and pulled me closer to him. He grabbed me by my hips and hiked up my dress just like he had done to my Barbie doll earlier. Then he pulled my panties down and began licking me between my legs. It did tickle but again, no laughter. I knew what he was doing was wrong. He picked me up by my waist and laid me on the bed, which couldn't have been too hard to do. I weighed less than 100 pounds. He continued to put his mouth on me while I stared at the ceiling and kind of zoned out. I noticed a water stain and thought it looked like a dried-out puddle of mud. I traced the brown outline with my eyes and wondered how it got there. It looked like something that you'd see outside on the ground. Instead, it was inside grandma's house on the ceiling. It felt like the whole world was upside down. The next thing I remember was feeling pressure on top of me and between my legs. With his face close to mine, I could smell the stench of stale wine on his breath. He started mumbling and complaining.

"Shit! It won't fit. I need some Vaseline or something."

As he stood up, I saw his penis. It was erect. I realized that was what he was trying to put inside of me. I didn't move. I was just waiting for it all to be over with. He rummaged around the room, opening and slamming dresser drawers closed looking for some kind of lubricant, I guess. It may have been a few seconds or a few minutes, but the pause was long enough for my hero to come save the day.

"What is all that racket?" a voice said as the bedroom door swung open.

"Grandma!" I was so relieved to see her, I started to cry.

Lester was literally caught with his pants down. His eyes became the size of golf balls when he saw grandma standing there.

"You dirty motherfucker!" grandma screamed and started swinging her purse at Lester like it was a sword.

Lester dodged her blows like Floyd Mayweather while pulling up his pants and ran out of the room. I got up off the bed and raced over to grandma.

"Stay here," she commanded as she quickly exited the room behind Lester.

I stood by the door ear-hustling. All I heard was lots of yelling on one end and a bunch of "I'm sorry" on the other.

Then I heard Lester say, "Wait! No, no, no…you ain't gotta do all that. I'm leaving. Help! Help!"

I heard that screen door open and shut. It was a sound you couldn't mistake for anything else. It opened and closed a second time and then Bang! Bang! Bang! And those weren't fireworks I heard.

Shannon came running into my room and asked, "What happened?"

I just told her, "Grandma and Uncle Lester had a fight."

She just looked at me and asked, "Are you alright?"

I nodded my head, yes.

"Good," she said and went back to her room.

A few minutes passed and grandma was back inside checking on me.

"Are you okay, baby?" she asked as she took me in her arms and held me tight.

"Yes. I'm okay, Grandma," I replied.

"I'm so sorry, baby. I'm so sorry. I should have never left you alone in the house with him." She rocked me back and forth. "It's not your fault, okay? He's a sick man. Something's wrong with him."

"It's okay, grandma. He just touched me." I tried to minimize the extent of what happened to ease any kind of guilt she may have felt.

"He shouldn't have done ANYTHING to you, baby, and I promise you he won't ever touch you again. There are some men in this world who you just can't trust," she said and kissed me on my forehead.

Grandma was right about two things. Years passed, and I never did see Lester again. He was still around, of course, but he avoided my grandmother and me like we were bill collectors. I also learned to be cautious about trusting men because this situation with Uncle Lester wasn't the first time an older man touched me inappropriately.

Grandma had no idea I had been down that road before, probably a year or two earlier during another summer in Tuscaloosa, where people let their guard down because everyone is so friendly and full of Southern hospitality. As a result, I was able to get away with things in Tuscaloosa that I would never be allowed to do in Atlanta. For example, I could walk to the store by myself in Alabama. I think I started going to the corner store by myself when I was about 7 or 8 years old. Everybody knew who I was and who my grandmother was. As a child, I got my steps in every summer going back and forth to the store, to my friend's house or to my grandmother's apartment buildings. It was at those apartment buildings when I first got approached by an older guy. My guess is he was in his 20s, but I know for sure he was one of grandma's tenants. I saw him paying her rent at the house before.

"Hey, Ms. Leatha's girl! What you doing over here?" he asked. He was tall and thin, wearing a red tank top showing off his well-defined muscles.

"Nothing. Just looking for my friends," I answered.

"Well, let me help you find him."

I agreed to let him assist in my search. He asked me a bunch of questions while we walked around the neighborhood. Eventually, I found my friends and he went about his business. I thought he was a really nice guy. I would see him quite often when I walked over to the apartment complex.

"Hey Shermie, with your pretty self," he would say whenever he saw me. It was almost a part of my daily routine. If I'm being honest, I liked the attention he gave me. Then, on one of the hottest days of the summer, I ran into him and he asked me if I wanted to go up to his apartment for some Kool-Aid. It didn't seem like a bad idea because I couldn't find my friends anyway. It might have been too hot even for them to be outside.

We went up to his room, and that's basically what it was, a room. It was an apartment building but there were about 10 to 12 "rooms" inside. There was a closet, a sink, and a small kitchenette in his unit. He told me the bathroom was down the hall, but we had to share it with the other tenants on his floor. The layout was a decent-sized rectangular space. He used a bedsheet for a curtain on the one window in the room. The window also held his air conditioner unit. He turned it on for us right away and the breeze made his bed sheet curtain rise up into the air like a ghost. In his room was a twin bed, just like the one I had in grandma's house and a little card table next to it with a lamp sitting on it. He went into the closet and pulled out two folding chairs for us to sit in. He placed them by the card table and put his lamp on the floor.

"You like red Kool-Aid?" he asked me.

"Yes. That's my favorite," I told him.

He opened up the smallest refrigerator I'd ever seen in my life and pulled out a full, plastic container of Kool-Aid like it hadn't been touched yet. He grabbed two, small glasses and set everything down on the table. He poured a glass for me. It was clearer than the Kool-Aid grandma made. Hers used to be cloudy from all the extra sugar she added. His mix was still good though, and most importantly it was cold.

"It's good ain't it? Damn, it's still hot in here. I'm taking this shirt off," he said as he revealed his chest to me for the first time. "You can take yours off too if you want."

"No. I don't want to," I insisted.

"That's okay, little lady. You're sexy with or without clothes on, I'm sure." He stood up and leaned over me. "Can I give you a kiss?"

He held my chin with his thumb and index finger. It reminded me of how my father would give me kisses when I was a small child. I didn't say yes, but I didn't say no either. He placed his lips on mine. Things escalated quickly, but only to a certain point. He rubbed all over my body from my budding breasts to my behind. He guided my hands showing me where to rub on him. He ended up fingering me and pleasuring himself, but he never tried to penetrate me with his penis. He had plenty of opportunities if he wanted to because I would stop by his room on many occasions the rest of that summer.

Those two early experiences ignited a sexual flame in me at an early age. I had a cousin around my same age that I began fooling around with. We'd explore each other's bodies and kiss and hunch on each other when we were alone. It felt like a safe space for both of us at the time. As a result of the molestation I had experienced and my natural curiosity, I lost my virginity four days before my 13th birthday. I learned to compartmentalize and separate sex from feelings. For a long time, I found myself attracted to older men. It would take time and a therapist to help me heal from that early childhood trauma.

> *I learned to compartmentalize and separate sex from feelings.*

PURPOSE NOTE

Trauma can cast long shadows, but confronting it brings light and understanding. As a young adult, I didn't understand the need to protect myself from predators, which left me confused about boundaries and the difference between love and false intimacy. The violation I experienced revealed the gaps in my understanding of self-protection, showing me how deeply rooted my lack of boundaries was. My journey has taught me that while pain can distort our perceptions, it can also reveal where we need to heal. Speaking the truth, even when it feels unbearable, was my first step in reclaiming power. Healing is not about forgetting the past but about recognizing its impact and building the strength to move forward with greater clarity. This process is ongoing and with each step, I find more light and more purpose.

3

When Everything Changes

But I was built to last.
SHERMIE HARGROVE

$\mathcal{N}$othing lasts forever and forever never lasts too long. Change is like the wind blowing flowers off a magnolia tree, not caring where they land. Just as my flower began to blossom, the winds came for me. I was getting older, but my grandmother was too. I always knew her to be so vibrant and feisty while I was growing up, but time spares no man or woman. Granny began getting sick. She was in her 80s before she began to falter. There wasn't a true condition she was suffering from, or at least not one that she disclosed to us. She had just gotten old and lost some of the pep in her step. She attributed it all to old age. My seasonal visits turned into weekly visits, and eventually, those turned into visits in the hospital and nursing home.

My dad had gotten custody of me and my brother years earlier, so he was our primary custodian. Our primary stability, however, came from grandma's house in Tuscaloosa. Once that was taken away from us, it felt like we were living in a house made of straw. My mother was deceased and my father battled a big, bad wolf that was constantly huffing and puffing at our door. Dad had become addicted to smoking crack cocaine. Of course, that complicated our living situation even more. Somehow, dad kept it together enough for us to always keep a roof over our heads. I don't ever remember being threatened by the possibility of homelessness, but we never stayed in one place too long. We moved around a lot. Out of necessity, I turned into a social butterfly because I was constantly switching schools and having to make new friends. Although it was frustrating, I became very adept at acclimating to any situation I encountered. We were something like nomads, even though dad was a functioning addict and his wife had her own business.

Daddy had this thing with cars. He used to repossess them, but not in the usual way. No tow truck, no drama. Plus, it was less expensive that way on both ends. Just him, a Slim Jim, and his skill. He worked for small companies, picking up cars when people couldn't pay. That was his life for a long time. My stepmom AJ, on the other hand, was something else. She owned a modeling agency and had a cosmetics line named after her daughter, Charlotte Cosmetics. People always said she was beautiful—tall, long hair, the whole package. And my dad? He was the kind of man who turned heads, always charming, always excited. He could have been a politician in another life, or an R&B singer if he'd had a voice.

Dad and AJ's relationship was toxic, and I found myself caught in the middle. My stepmother harbored a resentment toward me that I wouldn't fully understand until much later. It turns out, I bear a striking resemblance to my birth mother, and that's where the friction began. In his younger days, my dad was a wild spirit—a true charmer with a magnetic presence. His confidence and bravado led him down a reckless path. He fell in love with my mother and together, they decided to build a life. Dad always spoke of his "Queenie" with pride, sharing stories that portrayed her in a complex light, including that she was once a prostitute—a claim I never validated with anyone else. I wasn't sure I was ready to explore that narrative, and I never had the chance to ask him to elaborate. Now, I am committed to uncovering my mother's story because I know that in doing so, I will also learn more about my own. Although he had other children

> *Now, I am committed to uncovering my mother's story because I know that in doing so, I will also learn more about my own.*

before my brother and me, he was determined to create a family with us. I often wondered why he didn't choose to raise his other boys. Their stories were just whispers in the background of my childhood. It wasn't until my 40s, shortly before or after dad's death, that I finally met them.

After my parents moved to Atlanta, AJ entered the picture. She was the other woman, another reason I think she was never kind to me. I'm not one hundred percent sure, but I believe she was another one of the girls he was pimping. She always wanted to take my mother's place. The animosity she had for my mother was passed down to me. I remember vividly one of my birthdays after my mother passed away. I had just returned from Six Flags White Water with my cousin and stepsister. I hurt my leg on a waterslide called the Dragon's Tail. It didn't look much different than a water-based version of those giant potato sack slides you find at a carnival but after traveling down a slide with a plateau, I went airborne! I met the minimum height requirements, but I think I was so skinny I didn't have enough weight on me to hold me down. I couldn't have been in the air for more than a second, but I panicked and flailed and landed awkwardly on my leg. By the time my cousin Charlotte and I got home, I was moving slowly. AJ and her friends had cooked for me, and as they started singing "Happy Birthday." AJ got upset because I wasn't moving fast enough to get downstairs. I didn't understand why they didn't wait for me to come downstairs in the first place, but she interpreted my actions as being disrespectful. When I finally made it down, she was mean, making snide comments.

"We done slaved in this kitchen all afternoon for you, and you just gonna take your little time getting down here, huh? With your spoiled ass," AJ sternly scolded me.

I don't know where my dad or brother were, but I scanned the entire kitchen and living area looking for them. They were nowhere to be found. I felt completely alone and targeted. In my head, everyone was siding with her.

"Mmm hmm," I heard her girlfriends say as they nodded in agreement.

"Teenagers!" Another smirked.

With all her friends egging her on and fueled from the alcohol that they had been drinking while preparing for my birthday party, she must have decided she was going to show out in front of them.

We were the last two to exit the kitchen. As everyone had their backs turned to us while pouring into the dining room, I felt AJ's hand press against the back of my head and forcefully slam me face-first into the back of one of the hard, wooden, dining room chairs. I felt a sting that numbed my lips. It made me think I lost a tooth.

"Ungrateful bitch," she whispered in my ear as she loosed my head.

"Daaaaddy!!!!" I yelled out in pain.

He was nowhere to be found in our house and on my birthday. Next, I called for my brother instead. "Jarvis!!!!!" He came flying down the stairs.

"What's wrong?" he asked me.

"AJ hit me in the face with a chair," I explained to him.

"What the fuck is wrong with you, stupid ass hoe???!!" Jarvis said as he went off on our stepmother.

I don't remember everything that went on after that, but it wasn't good. They didn't get into anything physical but I remember them going back and forth at each other.

While I was crying hysterically, I heard AJ yell out, "Get the fuck outta my house, nigga!"

The exchange was heated. I drowned out everything by covering both my ears with my hands and rocking back and forth, telling myself that everything was going to be alright. The end result was my brother moved out that night. I'm not sure if she made him move out or if he just said "Fuck it" and left on his own. I just remember he never came back to the house after that night.

At some point, my father finally got home for my birthday party. Not sure if he ever wished me a happy birthday that night, but I'm pretty sure he already knew there was a problem. Maybe he had talked to my brother before he got there. He asked me what happened. I told him everything that had taken place. I don't remember specifics but things got tense and an argument ensued. Still, my dad was as cool as the other side of the pillow. He didn't raise his voice. He didn't raise his hand. For a long time, I felt responsible for breaking up our family. My brother had moved out, and things between me and my step-sister changed. Charlotte didn't talk to me anymore. It could've been due to our 10-year age gap, but she started being mean to me, in my opinion. I only felt like I belonged when my dad was around. Despite the spotty relationship between me, my father, and his crack addiction, things must have still affected him though because eventually my stepmother and father went their separate ways.

Another unpleasant memory from my childhood that I reflect upon is riding around with my dad, visiting some rough neighborhoods. I could always tell when we were close to them. We'd see more and more people just hanging out in the street, especially young boys in front of apartment complexes and gathering at gas stations. I'd be riding in the backseat looking out the window and he'd tell me to lie down before we entered certain places. I'd hear the car door open and close as he got out of the car. There would be nothing but silence but it would never last too long. He'd always return to the car happy, whistling and singing. Before he started the car up again, I could see the flicker of a lighter illuminate the car interior. I'd hear the sound of him inhaling deeply and the flicker momentarily disappear. Sometimes I'd hear a snap, crackle, and pop, like when I pour milk over a bowl of Rice Krispies. Then I'd hear his exhale, "Wooooooooooooo...." and I'd see his broad shoulders immediately begin to relax and slump in the front seat. That smell though. That's something I'll always remember–a burning, chemical smell. After my dad got his head right, he would start to move slowly, talking sluggishly. He was just out of it man, but somehow we'd always make it home.

Home was a condo back then. One day I came home from school to find fire trucks everywhere. Our condo had caught on fire! Of course, my stepmother claimed it was my dad's fault. She said he passed out smoking a cigarette, and it fell on the carpet and started a fire. I don't know if that was true, but it seemed to be the final straw. After that, our family scattered. As mean and disruptive as she was, seems like my stepmother was helping hold everything together for us. Once AJ was out of the picture, I stayed with different friends while my dad drifted around. The first person to take me in was my best friend's mom. I stayed with Misty and her mom for some time and everything seemed cool. In fact, Misty and I are still friends to this day. Not sure what changed and when it did, but at some point Misty's mother was like "Come and get your child." By then, I had very limited options. My stepmother and stepsister were officially out of my life, and I wouldn't see them again until my brother passed away.

By 11 years old, I was living out of hotels with my dad. He was staying at a hotel with a woman and her child. Her daughter was much younger than me, and they'd make me babysit her while they would go out to get high. For no reason that I can figure out on my own, I found myself being mean to that little girl. Maybe it was resentment for everything I was going through and I took it out on her. It could have been because she was always crying and I didn't know what to do. I would feed her, but the crying only stopped momentarily. I'd try holding her and rocking her back and forth, but she still wouldn't stop crying. I think she just wanted her mother, and there was nothing I could do about that. Then one day, without any explanation from my father, the woman and her baby were gone. It was just me and dad again.

On one occasion, I found myself with my father getting ready for school in a McDonald's bathroom. He sent me to the women's restroom to wash up and brush my teeth. I felt a little embarrassed getting dressed in a public bathroom. It felt like the women who came in while I was there were judging me.

Fortunately, I attended a school with teachers and women who looked out for me. They genuinely seemed to care about my well-being. One aid always made sure I had what I needed to participate in field trips and somehow, my way was always paid. I also had all my school supplies, which made me feel supported and cared for. I always received love from those around me. One of my teachers would often have an apple or something else for me to eat if I was hungry, and I often wondered if the snacks she gave me were gifts from her other students. One day, I couldn't take it anymore. I woke up bleeding and in a panic. It was my first period. I didn't even want to tell my dad what was going on. That same day, I called my Aunt Roz, who lived in Dallas. She was the closest resemblance of stability I could think of. A few days later, dad and I were on the road to Dallas, where I started living with Aunt Roz. Looking back now, I understand that the connection I felt with Aunt Roz was rooted in the things I saw in her that reminded me of my grandmother. It was why my soul connected with her at such an early age. Although my family was closer to her brother Uncle John—because that's who we would visit most when we were in Dallas—it was something about Aunt Roz that resonated with me. She was always a well-put-together woman with a clean home and a regal aura. She appeared to be very boss-like, and her spirit led me to reach out to her.

My dad was supposed to come back for me at the end of the school year. That would give him plenty of time to get his act together and find some permanent housing for us. He never came back for me. Just like AJ and Charlotte, I didn't see him again until my brother passed away. Aunt Roz, Uncle John, and my dad used to run together as kids. Since Dad was an only child, they were like siblings to him. My father had no relationship with his biological father. In fact, he didn't even know who he was. Then when his mother passed away, he was raised by his Aunt Dear given my dad's mother Sherry passed when he was young. That's actually how I got my name, Shermie. It was a mix between my grandmother's name Sherry and my father's name Jimmie. It's funny how dad and I had similar childhoods, with both of us being raised by our aunts who treated us as if they were our mothers.

I remember when Aunt Dear first got sick. Dad didn't hesitate at all. The next thing I knew, we were packed up and headed to Dallas to live, including AJ. Dad and AJ had gotten married while we were there. I completed a full school year in Texas while Dad remained by Aunt Dear's side every day until she eventually passed away. I guarantee I would have completed several years of school in Dallas had Aunt Dear lived longer. My daddy was not going to leave her. I realized just how important Aunt Dear was to my father, and a part of me longed to have a relationship similar to that.

Luckily I recalled my early visits to Dallas to see Aunt Roz. She seemed very fond of me. That's why I felt comfortable asking her if I could stay with her. Besides, I had done a year of school in Dallas previously.

Living with Aunt Roz was different. She was a cover girl, always dressed to the nines, and her home was always immaculate. Having a place where I felt stable was a relief. Aunt Roz moved us into a duplex in DeSoto, Texas, where I shared a room with her youngest daughter, Bebe. We got along okay, but things were never easy. Bebe was a few years older than me and going through her rebellious stage. I think she was acting out at the time because Aunt Roz and her dad were getting a divorce. After 17 years of marriage, the world Bebe once knew was ending. It was a lot for her to handle, and it led to trouble for both of us. One night we snuck out of the house together and took her mom's car. We were joyriding and ended up getting in an accident. We were both okay and the damage wasn't too bad, but I was shocked by Bebe's reaction. That night she decided she wasn't going back home. She wrote her mother a letter about the car, but never mentioned that I was with her. She always looked out for me and protected me like a big sister. I was really saddened by her leaving. In addition, regardless of my dad's imperfections, I loved and missed him. I wished he would have stayed in Texas with me. I also missed my brother's gentle spirit terribly.

Eventually, Aunt Roz moved us all into a bigger place. Although I couldn't have the best of both worlds, I was happy to be reunited with one. My brother came to live with us after he and my dad had an altercation. Supposedly, he kept asking my brother for money. My brother kept telling him no. My father ended up getting really frustrated. My brother said that dad snapped and grabbed an iron off the kitchen table and knocked him upside his head. He had to be about 17 at the time, which was still too young to be on his own. I was happy to have him with me in Texas. My brother was handsome and charming. People gravitated to him all the time. He easily made new friends in school. I loved it when he used to pick me up from school. All the girls liked him, and I would tell them all, ''That's my brother!" I absolutely adored him. He didn't stay long, but I cherished the time we had together. I'm not sure how he and my father reconciled, but Jarvis returned to Atlanta. Soon after, I fell into a spiral, acting out and feeling lost.

I became a little depressed when my familiarity was taken away from me. My father still wasn't able to care for me, and my brother was gone again. In an attempt to get Aunt Roz's attention, I took several Ibuprofen pills, hoping someone would notice the pain I felt from missing my dad and brother. I took just enough to make myself sick, not because I wanted to end my life but to numb the feeling of loss. I started acting out. I learned the art of sneaking out of the house from Bebe. I got caught several times, but Aunt Roz wasn't like grandma. I didn't get spankings. Instead, I was put on punishment. No TV, no phone, or sent to my room. Aunt Roz would buy me all kinds of things and then take them away as punishment, but none of those things mattered to me. Eventually, I was no longer afraid of getting caught. Later that year, I lost my virginity to the boy who lived across the street and was at least four years older than me.

I think it would have helped if Aunt Roz was more emotional. The things she did for me showed me she loved me. I even began calling her mom. Still, maybe I heard her say "I love you" twice during the time I stayed with her. I had all of these emotions that I didn't know how to deal with and wanted someone to talk to about them. Unfortunately, mom didn't come across as very approachable. That doesn't mean she didn't care, she just had a different way of expressing her affection. I think that's why she was always buying me things. Be that as it may, I couldn't fight the urge to express myself. A closed bedroom door wouldn't stop me. I began writing down my feelings and expressing myself on paper and sliding notes underneath my aunt's door. My technique worked and finally I was heard. It's something I still do to this day. Writing became therapeutic for me. I write to people when I'm hurt or upset to get my point across and try to avoid creating conflict.

Mom didn't know what to do with me herself, but she did know how to address the problem. Around that time, she decided it would be best if I started therapy. My first therapist was this white lady, but I barely spoke to her. In my mind, there was no way she could relate to me. Then I got matched up with a Black therapist named Keith, who got more out of me. He recommended a place called the Promise House, a program for troubled girls. I stayed there for about six weeks, learning about therapy, doing chores, and just trying to figure things out. It wasn't a negative experience, but I don't remember forming any real connections there.

> *The therapy helped me understand my pain, my abandonment issues, and how those things shaped me.*

The therapy helped me understand my pain, my abandonment issues, and how those things shaped me. But it took years for me to truly grasp the lessons. I was just moving forward, trying to survive. The way I showed up in relationships was a reflection of all the hurt I carried. After

I completed the program at Promise House, my brother came down to visit me. He was headed to the State Fair Classic to see the Grambling State versus Prairie View football game. Of course, I wanted to go to the game with my big brother! Mom said no, and I lost it. We had a huge argument. I may have been in my feelings when I said it, but I told her, "I don't want to live with you anymore! I want to live with my brother." I said the quiet part out loud and surprisingly, she agreed. I guess mom felt like she had already done everything that she could. I was at an age where she probably thought it was a better idea to choose her battles wisely, especially considering how things went with Bebe. So at 15, I moved back to Atlanta with my brother, who was 21. That move marked another chapter in my life, one filled with new challenges and heartaches, but it also set the stage for the woman I would become.

PURPOSE NOTE

As we grow, we often face moments when everything we thought we knew starts to shift. Change can be overwhelming, like a storm that leaves us feeling lost and exposed. Even when the world around us feels unstable, we discover something powerful within ourselves—a strength that helps us navigate the chaos. My journey taught me that home isn't just a physical place. It's the resilience we carry inside that helps us stand tall even when life throws us off balance. No matter how many changes come our way, we can learn to be strong and adaptable, just like a tree bending in the wind.

4

Am I My Brother's Keeper?

I would say so.
SHERMIE HARGROVE

$\mathcal{M}$oving in with my brother in Atlanta wasn't the exciting reunion I had envisioned. I hoped we would be a family again, just like those summers spent at grandma's house. While he was 21 years old and capable of making adult decisions—able to vote, join the Army, and buy cigarettes and beer—he still had the mindset of a young man trying to navigate his way through life. He wasn't just a boy without direction. He was taking on responsibilities, including mine, because I asked him to. He wouldn't dare deny his little sister. However, he was also a young man with access to money, which attracted women. Instead of spending quality time with me, he was always on the go. Though he had money, he was still searching for validation. To fill the void in his life, he surrounded himself with people and became the caretaker of many.

His house was bigger than any house we had lived in before, and he had several cars, all of them really nice. I'll admit it: I thought he was dealing drugs at first, but he had a different kind of hustle. He would change cars on a weekly basis. There would be a Beamer and a Benz in the driveway one week and a Cadillac and Corvette the next. There were Monte Carlos and Chevy box cars with BBS rims and kits that sat so low you weren't getting over a speed bump without scraping the bottom of your car. Jarvis worked at a car lot where he and some other guys flipped cars. That's when you buy a car at a low price and sell it at a profit. Technically, he wasn't doing anything illegal, but his boss was some Italian mobster-looking guy straight out of the movie *GoodFellas*. When my brother introduced me to him, he gave off con artist vibes. Even if he was crooked, my brother was not.

Even though my brother loved me, he lacked relatability for a teenage girl. Fortunately for me, he had a girlfriend at the time who took me under her wing. Her name was Nancy. She was right around my brother's age. I spent so much time with her over her house that people began to say we looked alike and thought we were related. We were becoming like sisters. In fact, once I began spending the night over Nancy's house, it seemed like I lived with her and her family instead of living with my brother.

The funny thing about all of this is that Nancy still lived with her parents. Correction. She lived with her parents, younger brother, and younger sister. I was the sixth mouth they fed. Lucky for me they didn't seem to mind. They quickly became like a second family to me. Of course, my brother noticed my absence, but it didn't bother him completely. He was never home anyway. He always had something to do or somebody to help out. We were similar in that sense. We both longed to be part of a family and treated our friends as such. Blood is thicker than water, but when you add some flour to that water it thickens real quick. That's what happened with me and Nancy. It also happened with my brother and his new associates. At times, we both benefited from those extended family relationships. Other times we'd have to learn the hard way that you can't trust everybody.

It was only a matter of time before Nancy ended up pregnant by my brother. I thought it would have been a happy time for them. I was excited about having a niece. My brother, on the other hand, was scared and acting funny.

"You know grandma would whup you if she was here and saw how you were acting!"

"Well, she ain't here, is she?" he said back to me with a major attitude. "And you're MY sister. Why are you taking her side? 'Cuz you basically live with her now?"

I thought becoming a father would slow Jarvis down at first, but I was wrong. I wanted us all to be one big happy family, something right out of the fairy tales. But it was business as usual to him. Fortunately, Jarvis eventually stood tall and began treating Nancy right. Plus, Nancy had me on her side as our bond grew stronger. I defended her and shielded her from my brother's immaturity and selfishness. As a result, our relationship deepened.

I told Aunt Roz about my current living situation. She was not pleased at all and demanded that I return back to Dallas to live with her. Honestly, I didn't want to go back. Nancy and her family became like a real family to me, but I had no choice. I was only 15. I couldn't make those kinds of decisions on my own yet. To complicate things even more, I had started a full-blown relationship with Nancy's little brother. He was a year younger than me. It was the first time I dated someone my own age. It was a completely inappropriate relationship with many challenges since I lived in the house with him and none of his family members knew what was going on between us. Nevertheless, after all I had been through, it felt nice to be with someone on my own terms who didn't manipulate me.

Despite everything I had going on in my little life, I returned to Dallas, where I re-entered therapy. I was meeting with the same therapist, Keith, again. Maybe I was talking a little more. After all, I was getting older and a little more mature, but I'm still not sure if I was getting anything out of therapy. My relationship with Aunt Roz was strained to say the least. We were civil and I appreciated the stability she offered me, but the distance between us even in her own house was palpable.

Still young in my decision-making abilities, I wanted to transfer high schools. The one I attended was predominantly white, and I wanted to be around people who looked like me. Then, to make matters worse, the small number of Black friends I had at my school were transferring to Carter High School in Oak Cliff. That's where it was at! I knew because my grades fell when I moved back to Dallas and had to attend summer school at South Oak Cliff High. I was mad I had to go to school in the summer, but I wasn't mad at all about being around my people. That summer was for the culture. I was intrigued by the fashion, the hairstyles, and the pro-Black mentality that was on full display every day on that bus ride coming and going to school. It was about this time people started calling me Mimi instead of Shermie. I liked hearing the name Mimi. I wasn't going to just let that experience slip away that easily.

I had an older cousin named Yolanda who lived on that side of town. I spent more and more time over her house until I eventually moved in with her and her husband. Yolanda was more like a cool older sister. Living with her was liberating. I could drink and have boys over without judgment. I still remember getting into that argument with Aunt Roz about going to the Bayou Classic with my brother. I never had those kinds of issues with my cousin Yolanda. With her, it was basically do whatever you want, just don't get arrested.

Living with Yolanda was the absolute best experience with one exception, her husband Kevin. Their relationship was toxic. Like my father, Kevin was constantly involved with other women, drugs, and overall chaos. One night, my best friend at the time, Moochie, came over to the house to spend the night. Yolanda and Kevin were both home with us that night. I thought Moochie would be okay, but Kevin made his move on her. They ended up sleeping together. Moochie was in her junior year of high school just like me and was 16 years old. The number of grown-ass men that I've come across in my life who've taken advantage of young, naive girls sickens me. I also couldn't believe that Moochie let him. But Kevin wouldn't get off that easy. Just like grandma walked in on Uncle Lester abusing me, Yolanda walked in on Kevin and Moochie. All hell broke loose. The fallout after that night was massive. Yolanda still stayed with Kevin despite what he had done, but Moochie never looked at me the same after that. She didn't blame me for what happened. It was consensual sex. But she didn't feel her best friend protected her from that situation. Honestly, she was right. In my head, I went as far as blaming her for what happened. I chose to ignore what Kevin did because he was family and at that point in my life, I put family over everything because I didn't want to be alone. I never even told Aunt Roz what happened. Not long after that, I moved back in with Aunt Roz. It was my senior year of high school and mom wanted me home.

> *I put family over everything because I didn't want to be alone.*

Despite everything, I still cared for Yolanda. Her home was chaotic, but it was also a place where I could escape and I was still welcome.

Another turning point in my life came after a high school football game. Some of my girlfriends and I had stopped by Yolanda's house and were waiting for some guys to come over. Unexpectedly, my aunt and her friend frantically showed up on the doorstep of Yolanda's house. I was trying to think what could I have possibly done to get my aunt to get out of bed and come all the way across town to get me. I was thinking she was just tripping at first, but I knew something was really wrong when she grabbed me by my hands. She was never touchy, feely like that, and then I noticed her hands were shaking uncontrollably.

"I'm so sorry, baby. Jarvis is gone. He was in a terrible car accident," she said and gave me a hug like the one I'd been looking for the whole time I'd been living with her. We held each other and cried together.

The loss was devastating. In the car accident, not only did I lose my brother, but his close friend was in the car with him and died as well. The other car involved in the accident carried a married couple who didn't survive either. The following day, Aunt Roz and I flew to Atlanta to make arrangements.

PURPOSE NOTES

This chapter reflects a deep desire to belong and to find stability within family ties, whether through blood relatives or those we choose along the way. The bonds I formed with people like Nancy, her family, and even Yolanda, were born from a need to fill the void left by the instability in my life. These connections, though powerful, were often shaped by trauma, creating relationships that weren't always healthy but offered the comfort I craved.

Losing my brother was a devastating blow, not just because of his absence but because he represented a piece of the family I yearned for. His passing intensified the void I already felt, a reminder that no matter how hard we try to hold on, life's circumstances are often beyond our control.

Through these experiences, I've come to realize that trauma can bond people in ways that feel like love but might only serve to deepen our wounds. My journey has taught me that true family isn't just about who's there during the hardest moments, but about finding healing within ourselves, rather than relying on others to fill our emptiness. The purpose I found through these experiences is this: It's important to build connections, but even more important to seek wholeness within so that the love we share with others can be grounded in strength and not survival.

5

Losing Familiarity, Again

The first broken piece
SHERMIE HARGROVE

Jarvis was no longer with us. His life shattered, but there were pieces of him left behind. Through those pieces, I put my brother back together again in my mind. When my aunt and I arrived in Atlanta, I got to meet my niece, Kayla, for the first time. She was five months old. When Nancy handed her over to me to hold, I couldn't stop looking her in the eyes. They were so very familiar to me. I'd seen them thousands of times already growing up with Jarvis. It was almost like getting to look at him one more time. I also had a five-year-old nephew. My brother and his girlfriend had him when they were 16. That boy had his spirit. It was easy to see Jarvis in him. What I wasn't aware of until Nancy told me about it was that my brother left this earth with one on the way. He had gotten another woman pregnant, and she was due any day. In fact, I was told the baby might be here before we bury my brother. I had hoped it was a boy born on the day of my brother's funeral. That would be like my brother was born again but instead, it was a beautiful little girl named Leslie. It hurts to know that her dad never got a chance to lay eyes on her.

Although I was thankful for my brother's legacy, I wasn't as happy about all the drama left here on earth for us to deal with. At the time of his death, Jarvis wasn't seeing Leslie's mother. He was living with another girl. In fact, he didn't stay with any of his children's mothers. He was living with two of his home-boys and a childhood girlfriend of his that he was close with named Marlene in an eight-bedroom mansion that had a pool. Obviously, this created a lot of tension between the women in my brother's life. I was closest to Nancy, and I took on more of a diplomatic position as my goal was to make sure all of them remained in my circle. I wanted to ensure that my nieces and nephew had a relationship with each other.

Things were chaotic, to say the least. Aunt Roz took the lead and tried to get everything organized for the memorial. Immediately she ran into issues. First, we couldn't find my brother's wallet. We needed his ID. They said his identifi-cation wasn't on him at the scene of the accident. Aunt Roz figured Marlene would find it at home, but she never did. The way my brother rolled, I'm sure there was a wad of cash in his wallet. I thought maybe someone on the scene took it, but why not just take the cash? Mom didn't think anything of it. She just handled business. Her solution to the problem was to shut everything and everyone down.

Her answer to anything was always "No." She was like an IRS auditor. She had no heart, and she didn't care about your feelings. She had a job to do.

"Can I get Jarvis' jewelry? I want to give it to his son one day."

"No."

People close to Jarvis wanted his furniture for their apartment.

"No."

"What are you gonna do with all his cars? I could take one off your hands."

"No."

Mom was all business, but she got it done. She didn't gain any new fans through the process, but she got my brother's affairs in order and laid him to rest properly.

The day of my brother's funeral was the first time I had seen my dad since he dropped me off in Dallas when I was 12 years old. He was in bad shape–emaci-ated, disheveled, and in need of a haircut. Still, he managed to put on a suit and tie out of respect for his baby boy. I noticed his neck leaning to the left. It was crooked and he couldn't seem to straighten it up. The rumor was that after he heard about Jarvis' death, they found him laid out in the middle of the street trying to get run over by a car. There's no telling what he could have done to himself to injure his neck.

I really wasn't sure where my father and Jarvis stood at the time of his death. They had reconciled from the physical altercation they'd had years earlier after my brother left Dallas. But since I had been estranged from my father and Jarvis never mentioned him, I didn't know if things had changed. My own relationship with my brother had been strained since I moved in with Nancy and her family. We still talked, but not with the closeness we once shared. I'll admit I felt some kind of way as people shared stories at the funeral saying they had just spoken to him the night before or the last time he saw them he told them how much he appreciated them. Sometimes people say when you're getting ready to leave this earth you attain this sense of humility and share those final moments with the people around you. That's something I never got from my brother before the end. We hadn't spoken in weeks and the last time I heard his voice, I didn't hear him say "I love you." I felt cheated, and it still affects me to this day.

> *Sometimes people say when you're getting ready to leave this earth you attain this sense of humility and share those final moments with the people around you.*

When people unexpectedly reach out wanting to have deep conversations or express love, I can't help but feel a sense that something ominous is about to happen. Right before my brother passed, people described him as different, lighter, as if he was making peace. My brother wasn't usually very talkative, but they said he was unusually chatty, almost as if he was touched by some spirit. But I can't help but wonder why that spirit didn't move him to call me. I've asked myself that so many times. I was at Yolanda's that day, and I keep thinking that if I had been home, we would have talked. Maybe he did call Aunt Roz's house. Seemed like I was the only one who ever answered the phone there. No caller ID. No cell phones. I don't even know how we existed as a people at the time. If I'd been home, I know we would have been chatting like usual, but I wasn't there. I might have missed his call. It's hard to say, but the thought lingers.

Ashes to ashes and dust to dust. After the dust settled and my brother was at rest, mom and I returned to Dallas. By the time we got home, something changed in me. I realized I needed to stop giving my aunt a hard time. Watching how she handled everything—taking care of business, being there for me and my brother—made me see how much she truly had my back. She became my person, the one I could always rely on.

Not long after I was back in Dallas, it seemed like high school graduation day snuck up on me. I graduated and got a job at Southwestern Bell, and started working in an office. Believe it or not, I was a corporate professional! I loved being in a corporate setting, and I lasted at that job for some time. Then mom and I got into it about something. Being spiteful, I quit on the spot. In an even more impulsive action, I decided to move back to Atlanta.

I desperately wanted to reconnect with my nieces and nephews, to be a part of their lives and carry on my brother's legacy. I moved back and became room-mates with Nancy once again. We got an apartment together, and I found a job at Equifax. Corporate life was working out for me. Things were going well. The only distraction I had to deal with in Atlanta was that my dad was incarcer-ated at the time. He didn't do anything major. He just had one too many drug possession arrests so the judge decided he needed to sit down somewhere for a little bit of time. When he was released, he came to live with me and Nancy. That was when I found myself in the unfamiliar role of caring for him. Atlanta was still his city, so he wasn't around much, but he had a special bond with his granddaughter, my niece Kayla, which meant a lot to Nancy and me.

Everything seemed to be fine until Nancy met her now-husband. He quickly became a fixture in our lives, almost like a third roommate. It was like she went out one night and met him, and he hasn't left her side since. Tensions rose when I felt he should contribute to the rent, especially since he was always there.

"Your daddy doesn't pay any rent," was Nancy's response.

Nancy and I nearly came to blows over it, and the issue became a defin-ing moment in our relationship. I had stood by her side through all the drama with my brother, but she had her man's back over mine. Although we eventu-ally made up, things weren't ever the same. I had lost my closest companion to her new relationship. No more road dawg. No more ride or die. Eventually, I decided to move back to Dallas. I stayed with mom for a while before getting a job and my own place. Then one day at a gas station, I met a cute guy who pumped my gas and asked for my number. We started dating and within three months, I found out I was pregnant. We weren't on the best of terms when it happened. We might not have even officially been together. Truthfully, our relationship was shaky and honestly, if I hadn't gotten pregnant, I doubt we would have stayed together. We didn't know each other well, but we decided to keep the baby. He was excited and so was I, but my family didn't share our enthusiasm.

Of course, mom in particular did not approve and was not supportive. She subtly suggested that I should consider an abortion, but I was determined to keep my baby. Even though many of my friends had already had children, my pregnancy seemed to shock everyone. It felt like I had let down the people closest to me, but I knew I wanted to have this baby. I gave birth to my son, Tavaris, and lived with my mom again. Despite her being discouraging in the beginning, she was a tremendous help in raising him. My child's father proposed to me after we had our son. I wanted to give us a family, so I said yes.

As time went on, the relationship between Yolanda and Kevin remained toxic and I would find myself in the midst of confusion again. Around the same time, my relationship with my child's father began to deteriorate as well. He cheated on me more than once and after the second time, I knew he wasn't the one for me. Breaking off our engagement and moving out wasn't as hard as I thought it would be. My dad had moved in with me, my child's father, and my son. Eventually I moved, but my father stayed for a while. He and my ex developed their own relationship and dad formed his own opinion of my baby's daddy. He eventually married the woman he was with when he cheated on me and had two more children with her.

I ended up staying temporarily with Yolanda. It wasn't a big deal to her, but Yolanda was never really the problem. At the time, Kevin and I were getting along fine, but things took a disturbing turn one day. I had dropped my son off at daycare. Kevin and I were alone in the home, which wasn't unusual, but then Kevin came into my room while I was lying in bed. He climbed into bed with me, asking what I was doing. I was stunned, freaked out, and immediately knew things were ruined. Why would he try me like that? He had never done anything like that as long as I had known him. After all that shit we went through with my friend in high school, how could he do this to me? I was only 21, and I didn't know how to handle it. I called my child's father and told him what happened. He urged me to leave and to tell Yolanda. I told him I would tell her but based on our past history regarding Kevin, I knew she wasn't going to do anything.

When Yolanda came home, I told her what Kevin had done, and she confronted him. Although I wasn't comfortable staying there anymore, I felt torn about how to proceed. Kevin later claimed that I had given him some sort of signal, but I knew that was a lie. Things were tense between Yolanda and me for a while. We eventually got past it, even though our relationship never fully recovered. We continued to hang out, but there was always an underlying weirdness.

Along with everything happening at Yolanda's home, I was having troubles of my own. My ex had become increasingly absent from Tavaris's life after his marriage. His new wife, who was later diagnosed with bipolar disorder, didn't like me. She didn't trust him to be a father to his son due to her own insecurity of how she started the relationship in the beginning. He pulled away from his responsibilities as a father. For about five or six years, he was completely out of our lives, leaving me to raise Tavaris on my own. But I never truly felt alone because I had a wonderful support system—my aunt, friends, and a community that surrounded us with love. One thing I was determined to provide for my son was stability, something I lacked growing up. I made sure he stayed in the same school district throughout his education, so he never had to deal with the instability of constantly moving. Even when his father reappeared after years of absence, I didn't try to control their relationship. I wanted Tavaris to have the opportunity to know his father, and I never stood in the way of that.

> *One thing I was determined to provide for my son was stability, something I lacked growing up.*

My 20s were dominated by motherhood. Then when TJ was two, I met Donald at a nightclub. He was a few years younger than me, but we clicked instantly. We moved in together quickly, maybe after just three months. I fell hard for him. At first, Donald wasn't physically abusive, but there were warning signs. He had a nasty side that came out when things didn't go his way—little things like pinching me when he was upset. I didn't recognize it as abuse back then. But Donald was also a cheater, and I caught him more than once. We were on a constant rollercoaster, breaking up and getting back together. We even planned to have a baby, but when I got pregnant, he started to waver. He would say things like, "I'm not sure I'm ready to have a kid." The idea of being a single mom again with two different baby daddies at just 22 scared me, so I ended the pregnancy. Then I found out another girl was pregnant by him too.

We set up a trap to catch him in the act, and it worked. But instead of confronting him, I ended up turning on the girl. She told me how and where they would hook up at his security job. I was on board with what she was saying until I found out she'd been in my house. He flipped it on her asking why I would team up with her and asked if she told me she was in my house. My house?! Well, that had never come up. The truth was it was never really about her, though. It was always about him and the hold he had on me.

We broke up, but I kept taking him back. The first time Donald hit me, I was in shock. It was over something trivial, and I didn't even see it coming. I wanted to hang out with my friends, and one of the girls was gay. He was questioning if I was attracted to her and if I wanted to be with her. I didn't know why that would even be a thought in his mind. In the heat of the moment, I told him he sounded stupid and then it happened. He slapped me. Instead of leaving, I stayed. We never talked about it, never addressed it. I knew from past conversations that Donald's father abused his mother. He promised me he would be different, but he was the same as his dad. Donald's drinking got worse over time, and the abuse escalated.

Toward the end of our relationship, the worst incident happened at a Christmas party in Austin with my coworkers. We rode in the car with them. The one driving was all over the road and Donald gave me a look questioning why we were in the car. He was very irritated by the entire situation of having to ride with anyone at all. We reached our hotel and all went to our rooms to change into our Christmas attire for the evening. My coworkers were from Austin and were trying to find the event venue. Everyone began to get confused and Donald was ready to leap in when I let him know calmly to hold on. They knew what they were doing.

Donald took my confidence as a threat. He hung back and when I tried to find out what was wrong, he told me very aggressively that I knew everything. We got inside and he started pinching me at this office party, so I moved away from him to keep from being noticed. The night progressed and he apologized to me so we ended on a good note. Everything was looking up until the car ride to Burger King. We all returned to the car and I laid my head on Donald's lap. The driver was my male coworker and his elbow slightly touched me. Donald was furious. He became loud and wanted me to tell him to move his elbow. When I told him to calm down, he chilled but I was so confused by all that he was doing. He was acting jealous over a coworker who was sitting with his girlfriend.

We made it back to the hotel and I was getting ready to take off my clothes for what I thought was an intimate moment and Donald pulled me by my ponytail. I could feel every bobby pin as the ponytail was ripped from my scalp. He choked me and pressed me up against a mirror. I knew my coworkers were in the next room and could hear us. I was embarrassed and ashamed. How was I even in this mess? I was trying to protect my image, but at what cost? The thought running through my head was, "Am I going to die?" He kicked me and even spat on me. My saving grace was he pushed me into the bathroom and told me to stay there and not to come out. It was my room but I stayed there until I heard him getting into the bed. I crawled up beside him and he had sex with me, and I just let him. It was an out-of-body experience. The next morning, it was like nothing had happened.I was riding back with my coworkers, hiding behind sunglasses, trying to act like everything was fine. We never mentioned it again, and I continued the relationship.

The abuse continued in small ways, enough that I started to believe it wasn't really abuse and that he was getting better. When it's never as bad as the first time, it seems like it's better. The beginning of the end was when my dad told me TJ, who was only 3, mentioned something about Donald. My dad asked me if Donald was putting his hands on me based on what TJ said. I denied it because I never wanted my son to see abuse but deep down, I knew better. The final straw came when Donald choked me again, this time picking me up by the neck and dropping me to the floor. I went to get take-out from Chili's and I wasn't ready to eat yet. I knew he was hungry and I made a small joke. He was not amused and began to choke me. The way I hit my head so hard, I realized I could have died. It was then I knew I had to get out for TJ's sake. I had something greater to live for–my son. He saw the abuse. I could no longer stay in the relationship.

I called my best friend, Sandy, and with her help, I moved out while Donald was gone. I changed my number and escaped that toxic relationship. Donald tried to come back a year later but by then, I was done. He was still the same person, and I wasn't falling for it anymore. The most important thing I learned from all of it was that I had to be strong for TJ. He was my reason for pushing through, for finding a way out, and for building a life where he could feel safe and loved.

The most unexpected blessing during that chaotic time was when my dad moved back in with me. It was the double-edged sword of a single mom. I was successful at work. I had my first leadership position as a director at my company. I was working 12 hours a day, six days a week, and making good money. I was running one of the largest campuses, but I needed help with my son. He needed care and I was always working. One day, my dad called to let me know he was hungry. I told him I would bring him something to eat and took TJ with me to take him a cheeseburger. When I saw dad, I noticed he didn't look well. The neighborhood he was living in was not the best and he looked cracked out. As we were leaving TJ said to me, "I thought we were going to see papa." My heart sank into my chest. My dad looked so bad that his own grandson couldn't recognize him. I had to do something. I called my dad and said, "I am going to get you tomorrow." I wanted to get him healthy and clean him up. My intention was to get my dad on the right path. I officially moved my dad into my home that day. I gave myself two weeks and he would be fine. Five years later, he was still there. He was the beginning of my caretaker journey. I wouldn't trade him for anything. He was such a present grandfather, and watching him with TJ was heartwarming. It felt like we had our own little family, just the three of us.

PURPOSE NOTE

I stayed in an abusive relationship, not realizing how much my understanding of love had been tangled up with survival. I think I confused intimacy with something else—something darker, more controlling. There were moments when I questioned everything, but I still held on, telling myself it was for the sake of love. In reality, I was holding on because I didn't know what else to do. The idea of being alone terrified me more than the pain I was enduring so I stayed. I stayed because I thought love was supposed to hurt, that maybe enduring was proof that I cared. What I didn't know then was that real love doesn't break you down, it builds you up. It took me time to understand that— and even longer to act on it.

Everything began to shift when I realized that my decisions were no longer just about me. My son was watching, absorbing everything, even in silence. His innocence made me see the situation with new eyes. I didn't want him to grow up thinking that this was what love looked like. I didn't want him to believe that pain and sacrifice were the price you paid to be loved or that silence was safer than speaking up. His presence gave me the courage to make hard choices. Leaving his father was difficult, but leaving the abusive relationship that followed was even harder. I was afraid of what life would look like on my own, but I feared even more what staying would teach my son. I wanted him to know love in its truest form, not the broken, painful version I had settled for.

It was my love for him that gave me the strength to go. I left, not just for me, but for him, so that he could see what real love and strength look like. It took everything I had, but I knew deep down that staying would have cost me even more.

6

50 First Dates

I thought I was ready.
SHERMIE HARGROVE

*M*uch of my dating life after Donald was like a roller coaster ride filled with many ups and downs and over in a matter of minutes. I took a pause from dating to heal from being in an abusive relationship. After about two years, I dated my best friend's brother. He was cool, but it felt like he was content with the status quo and never wanted to take things to the next level. It was the same thing with the guy I met while shopping at the grocery store. At first I thought I was special to him because he used to cook for me all the time. Come to find out, he did that for all his girls. It was an easy enough way to convince a woman to come over to his apartment. I met another man at the gas station. He insisted on paying when I was minding my business, just trying to fill up my gas tank. It took about three months for me to realize he had been gassing my head up the whole time I was with him. It felt like I was draining the swamp, kissing way too many frogs trying to find my prince. Due to all those dating disasters and disappointments, I eventually found myself in a very curious position. Because of that curiosity, I even kissed a girl.

Her name was Veronica. How I got connected with her was a bit tangled, like so many things in life. We met through two brothers. Before Veronica, I briefly dated another guy, although "dated" might be the wrong word because he was married the entire time. It sounds ridiculous now but at the time, I wasn't even sure how he was pulling it off. His wife didn't live in the same state, so he had this sort of freedom that made it possible for us to spend a lot of time together without raising suspicions. I'd go to his house and in those moments, it felt real. It felt like we were something. But of course, it wasn't real. If I'm being honest, I don't even remember all the details. What sticks out to me most is how I found out about his marriage—Veronica told me. She mentioned it casually like it was no big deal. "Oh, by the way, he's married," she said. It was a bombshell for me, but she didn't seem phased. She had her own complicated situation as she was married to his brother.

Veronica and I grew closer after that. Maybe it was because we were both looking for something more, something different. One night, after Veronica and her husband went through some kind of drama of their own, Veronica and I decided to go out together. It wasn't planned. It was one of those spontaneous nights where you just want to escape whatever mess your life is in. We drank a lot and by the end of the night, we were tipsy, laughing too loud, and feeling a kind of reckless freedom.

At some point, we met a guy. Thinking back on it now, I can't even remember who he was or how we met him. Maybe I had known him before, or maybe it was just one of those blurry, alcohol-fueled encounters that seem more significant at the moment than they actually are. What I do remember is that we went back to his house. It wasn't a good idea, but at the time, it felt fun, like we were living on the edge. The night took a turn when things became intimate between me and this guy. Veronica was there, just watching at first, and I couldn't shake the feeling that she was interested in me, not him. I had sensed it several times before. She'd make comments or touch me in ways that felt suggestive. She'd place her hand on my knee when we talked. Sometimes she'd put her hand around my waist as we walked. When I'd let her help with my makeup she would look at me in a way that let me know she thought I was beautiful.

That night, she didn't just watch. Veronica ended up getting involved. It wasn't about the guy anymore; it was about us—me and her. For me, it was the first time I'd been in a threesome. I didn't know how to feel about it in the moment, but I went with it. I didn't stop to question anything. I just let it happen. Afterward, Veronica and I talked about it, and she was clear—her feelings weren't for him. It had never been about him. She told me she had feelings for me and that she wanted to be with me. I didn't know how to react to that. I had never been with a woman before but I entertained the idea. I thought, "Why not?" So we started what you might call a relationship, although that word doesn't quite fit.

It didn't take long for me to realize that I wasn't comfortable with it. Veronica, on the other hand, was all in. She was the type of person who wanted to be open, public, about everything. She had a daughter and a son, and she didn't see any issue with our relationship being visible to them. I still only had TJ, and I wasn't ready to have that kind of openness in front of him. It just didn't sit right with me. I wasn't even sure why at the time. Was it because I wasn't comfortable with being in a same-sex relationship, or was it because of how I thought others would see me?

Veronica and I never had a big breakup moment. She never put hands on me like Donald. She didn't cheat on me like the others. We didn't even have a clear conversation about ending things. It was more like the relationship just fizzled out. She moved away, and the distance made it easier to let go of whatever it was we had. But if I'm being honest, I didn't really know how to break up with her. Ending relationships, cutting people off, has always been hard for me. I think it has to do with my own issues and my fear of abandonment. I don't know how to walk away from people without feeling like I'm abandoning them the way I've felt abandoned before. But at the same time, I knew I couldn't keep fostering a relationship I wasn't comfortable with, especially not from a distance.

After things ended with Veronica, I started questioning myself. I wondered, "Am I gay? Am I bisexual? Am I uncomfortable because of what other people would think, or because it's just not right for me?" It wasn't the first time I'd had those thoughts. But this situation with Veronica brought it to the forefront. I had to confront it in a way I hadn't before. In the end, after more reflection and a few other experiences, I realized that I wasn't gay. I wasn't bisexual, either. I'm what they call *fluid*. I've had moments in my life where I've explored different parts of my sexuality, but ultimately, I knew men were the direction I wanted to go in.

That relationship with Veronica, if you can even call it that, taught me a lot about myself. It made me face some uncomfortable truths and pushed me to question things I had always taken for granted about who I was. But it also helped me figure out what I didn't want, and sometimes that's just as important as knowing what you do want. Looking back, I don't regret it. Every experience, no matter how messy or confusing, has shaped who I am. That's something I've come to accept, even if I didn't understand it at the time.

Of course, the first man I dated after Veronica was secretly married. *"I sure know how to pick 'em,"* I said in my head. How does this keep happening to me? The signs were there, but I either missed them or chose to ignore them. This time, he was a truck driver. His name was Michael. My son and I had met him on the Pee Wee football field where Michael coached. That's how we got introduced, just a casual interaction between parents and coaches. I should have known better, though. Michael wasn't a complete stranger. He had a twin brother and another sibling and in that small circle of our kids and sports, it was easy to become familiar with the people who surrounded you.

At the time, I thought we were in a good place. We would go out in public together, meet up at games, and spend time with each other. It seemed like the beginning of something solid. But looking back now, the red flags were clear. For starters, I never once went to his house. Not once. But Michael, on the other hand, would come over to mine and even stay the night. I thought it was just part of the routine, like maybe his job as a truck driver made him too busy for me to come over.

It seemed like a normal enough relationship on the surface. We were out there on the field together, side by side, and no one suspected anything. He wasn't hiding me, or at least that's what I believed. Michael had kids too—a lot of them, in fact. Five or six, if I remember right. When he talked about his children, he often mentioned his ex-wife. That's all I knew—an ex-wife. No current wife, no present-day drama. But I should have known that someone with that many kids probably had more ties than he was letting on. Still, I convinced myself everything was above board. After all, he never once said he was married. Why wouldn't I believe him?

It wasn't until I met Kenetra that things started to unravel. Kenetra was dating Michael's brother, and we began to get to know each other because of our shared circles. We spent a lot of time in the same environment. As we got closer, she became one of my besties. There was also another woman in the group, Teresa, who was dating one of the other coaches. Teresa was a bit more reserved, but she seemed to know something I didn't. She would hang around, and I began to suspect that she was trying to tell me something without actually saying it. She didn't want to stir up trouble because of the close-knit connections between the men and our kids, but I started to catch on. I began to piece together what she wasn't saying aloud.

Teresa wasn't the only one who saw what was happening. My best friend Keeley and I joked about how we always acted like Inspector Gadget when it came to situations like this. We couldn't help ourselves. We had to figure things out. It didn't take long before I decided to follow Michael one day when he left my house. I needed answers. Keeley and I did some digging, too—looking up addresses, trying to put together the puzzle pieces. Eventually, we got what we needed.

I still remember that day. Keeley and I decided to go to Michael's house. We weren't sure what we would find, but we were determined to get to the bottom of it. We brought Keeley's dog as part of a ridiculous plan to act like we were looking for a lost pet. The excuse was thin, but it gave us a reason to knock on the door. My heart was pounding as we approached. A woman answered, and my stomach dropped. My worst fear was standing there right in front of me. I couldn't believe it. He was married. I lost all my nerves. I handed her a fake flier for a missing dog who ran away from home and asked her to call me if she saw him.

At first, I considered just confronting Michael directly but something in me snapped. I was younger then, and far less cautious than I am now. Instead of walking away, I went back to the woman's door. It didn't even cross my mind that she could have been dangerous or reacted violently. I had no idea who she was, but I felt this overwhelming need to tell her. So there I was, standing at her front door, telling her that I had been sleeping with her husband.

To my surprise, she invited me in, and we sat down and talked. She pieced things together for me, confirming everything I had feared. It was a sobering moment. I had no idea he was married, and I would never have willingly gotten involved in that kind of situation. But once I was in the middle of it, I had no one to blame but myself for letting it get that far. When I finally confronted Michael, he did what I expected him to do—he lied. Even after everything, he tried to deny the truth. He tried to convince me that if I took him back, he would leave his wife and family for me. I don't know if he was serious or just desperate to keep his double life going a little longer. Whatever the case, it was over. He had been living a lie, and there was no salvaging it.

The one good thing that came out of all of that was my friendship with Kenetra. She had wanted to tell me about Michael for a long time but was worried about how I would take it. She didn't want to ruin our friendship or cause problems in the family. In the end though, she became one of my closest friends, and that friendship lasted long after Michael and I ended.

Fast forward a bit, and you won't believe it, but it happened again. Another guy, another marriage I knew nothing about. At that point, I felt like I had a sign on my forehead that said, "Pick me if you are married." This time, the guy was African. His name was Tish and I met him through his brother, who did my taxes. I had gone to get my taxes done, and that's when Tish came on to me. There's a certain energy in African culture where things can move fast, and this was no exception. Tish was well off, and he didn't hold back when it came to showing it. He was paying my bills, taking me on trips, and showering me with gifts. I felt like I was part of a whole new world—fancy dinners, expensive shopping trips, and hanging out with his business partners and their girlfriends.It was glamorous, but there was something off. I couldn't quite put my finger on it at first.

We would spend nights out at clubs, living it up like we were carefree. I had no idea how he was pulling this off while being married. He never once gave any indication of having a wife, and yet, there we were, living this double life in public. One night, after we had spent an evening out with his crew, we came out of a nightclub to find all four of Tish's tires slashed. I couldn't believe what I was seeing. I looked around, trying to figure out what had happened, and then I saw her–his wife. She had found us, and she was furious. She started going off on him, and I was left standing there completely stunned. All this time he had been married, and I had no clue.

I confronted him, demanding to know what was going on. Instead of owning up to it, Tish started making excuses, saying the only reason he married her was for citizenship. I didn't believe it for a second. You don't slash someone's tires over a citizenship arrangement. This was much deeper than that. As if things couldn't get worse, his wife gave him his ring back right there in front of me. She threw it at him, and I just stood there, watching the whole thing unravel. Tish asked me to pull over after she left, and we ended up talking in some random field. He tossed the ring aside, telling me it was about me now, that he wanted to be with me. But I wasn't falling for it. He was willing to abandon his wife and child for me, and that wasn't the kind of relationship I wanted to be a part of. That was the end of Tish. I wasn't about to break up a family, even if I hadn't known I was doing it at first.

After that, I dated here and there, but I was cautious. The only men who had ever met my son, Michael, were Donald and my friend's brother. Donald was special because we had a deeper connection, but I wasn't bringing just anyone around my son. I didn't want to risk exposing him to that kind of instability. Around that time, I was working long hours at my job as a director managing one of the largest campuses for my company. It was my first leadership position, and I was putting in 12-hour days, six days a week. I was making good money, but looking back, I realize I was stretched too thin.

During that time, I met Van, who worked with me at ATI. It was hot and steamy at first. We would sneak around the office, meeting in each other's offices when no one was looking. He was the director of career services, and I was the director of admissions. We had fun, but things eventually fizzled out. It wasn't cheating or anything dramatic. It was just one of those things that didn't work out. Looking back, I realize I was probably too needy. Once again, I wanted more than a man was willing to give me. Van had a whole life outside of me, but I think I was so used to my past relationships moving so fast I thought he wasn't that into me.

The years seemed to blur together as I experienced a string of fleeting romances that always felt like they had potential, only to fizzle out when

I discovered the truth. Time and time again, I found myself falling for men who had already made their commitments elsewhere. It was as if I had unknowingly entered a secret club for women who dated men in half-relationships—half with me and half with someone else. It was disheartening, to say the least. I was just dating—here, there, everywhere—trying to find someone who would be wholly mine, but it felt like the universe had other plans.

> *Time and time again, I found myself falling for men who had already made their commitments elsewhere.*

That's when Casey came into the picture. He was different, or so I thought at the time. From the start, I knew he had a girlfriend, but at least he was upfront about it. Casey wasn't playing the "I'm single" game only to have a wife or girlfriend lurking in the shadows. He was a technologist with an infectious energy that drew people toward him—especially women. When he told me about his girlfriend, there was almost a sense of relief. "At least he's being honest," I told myself. In a twisted way, I appreciated his candor but that didn't make it any less complicated. Deep down, I knew I should've run in the opposite direction. My track record with men in relationships was already abysmal, and I had promised myself I wouldn't get caught up in another tangled web. But something about Casey made me hesitate. He kept coming back to me, like feeding a stray cat, and I couldn't help but wonder what that meant. Was there something about me that kept attracting men who were unavailable? Or was there something about me that made them want to stray from their current relationships?

It wasn't an earth-shattering connection between Casey and me. There were no fireworks, no deep, soul-baring conversations that made me feel like we were meant to be. It was just sex. Plain and simple. And yet, we held onto it. Off and on, for what felt like an eternity, we kept circling back to each other. A couple of years went by and it really hit me when Casey got married. Not to the girlfriend he had when I first met him, but to someone completely different. Once again, I was on the outside looking in, realizing that I had been playing a role in someone else's love story without ever being a main character. He didn't choose me. He never did.

Even after the wedding, our connection—if you could call it that—didn't just end. Casey would break up with his girlfriends, and we'd fall right back into the old pattern like nothing had changed. But it had. He would never bring me into the light. I was always just someone he was sleeping with, hidden away in the shadows, never to be acknowledged in public. I remember a moment of clarity one night, when he was single—at least that's what he told me. I couldn't take it anymore. I told him that I wanted more. I wanted something real, something that wasn't just about sneaking around and keeping things secret. I deserved more than to be someone's afterthought, their second choice when things didn't work out elsewhere.

His response was like a punch to the gut. He wasn't interested in a relationship, he said. He wasn't ready. And yet just like clockwork, a few months later I saw him with someone else. In another relationship. I couldn't wrap my head around it. How was it that he could so easily dismiss me, and then turn around and give someone else exactly what I had asked for? It felt like a cruel joke that life kept playing on me. After that, I ended it for good. Or at least, that's what I told myself. But, as with all things, life had a way of pulling us back together when I least expected it.

I ran into him again, this time after he had gotten married. I thought I had moved on. I had made peace with the fact that I wasn't and never would be the woman he chose. But seeing him again was like all the old habits kicked in. We fell back into the same routine, the same cycle of sneaking around and keeping things under wraps. It wasn't healthy, I knew that but somehow it felt comfortable, familiar even. By this point, though, I had moved back to Atlanta. Distance was supposed to be the thing that finally broke the pattern, the thing that kept us apart for good. For a while it did, but the memories of Casey lingered. It wasn't just him, though. It was the accumulation of all those men who couldn't give me what I wanted—what I deserved.

Looking back now, I see it all for what it was: A series of lessons I had to learn the hard way. I thought Casey was different because he was honest about having a girlfriend, but honesty didn't mean he was capable of giving me what I needed. Just because someone is upfront about their situation doesn't mean they're ready to change it or that they see you as anything more than a temporary distraction.

For years, I kept finding myself in these roles—playing the part of the woman on the side, the one men came to when they were bored or dissatisfied with their current relationships. It took a long time for me to realize that I was worth more than that, that I didn't have to settle for scraps of affection or half-hearted attempts at love. Casey wasn't my great love story. He wasn't even a footnote in what I now hope to be a bigger, more meaningful narrative. But he, like so many others, was part of a chapter that taught me something invaluable: I needed to stop accepting less than I deserved. I needed to stop falling for men who were already spoken for, emotionally unavailable, or just plain uninterested in giving me their all.

I'm saying all this to say that those years with Casey and the others weren't about love. They were about filling a void, about trying to find something in these men that I needed to find within myself first. It wasn't about them choosing me. It was about me choosing myself for the first time in a long time. That, as it turns out, was the most important choice I ever made.

PURPOSE NOTE

Life sometimes feels like a series of lessons disguised as disappointments. Each relationship I entered, whether short-lived or lasting longer than it should have, wasn't just a detour or a distraction. It was part of my journey, one that forced me to confront not just the lies others told me but the lies I told myself. These relationships reflected the spaces within me that were still searching for something real, for something lasting, and for something that made sense in the chaos of my life. I thought I was looking for love but really, I was searching for validation, for an answer to the question "Am I worthy of more?"

What I learned after so many missteps and heartbreaks is that our choices often mirror the parts of us that still need healing. The men I chose, the situations I found myself in, were a reflection of my own unhealed pain—my abandonment issues, my need for affection, and my fear of being alone. When

I finally saw that, the people I let into my life began to change, not because they were different but because I had changed.

This chapter isn't just about relationships. It's about self-awareness and recognizing that sometimes the real work of love begins with the love you offer yourself. It's about owning your past, even when it's messy, so you can claim the future that you truly deserve. As messy as my dating life was, each encounter gave me a clearer understanding of what I didn't want. More importantly, I gained a stronger sense of what I did want and need. In the end, it's not about how others define or treat us but how we learn to define and love ourselves through those moments of uncertainty.

Moving On

7

Changing cycles to save generations
SHERMIE HARGROVE

*I*n the midst of my career transition, I found myself taking a sharp turn that I hadn't anticipated. For most of my professional life, I had been in recruiting. I had grown comfortable with it but when I took a position at a for-profit college, things began to shift. I joined ATI, a college that was known for its fast-paced environment. It wasn't long before the inevitable happened: Layoffs. Though the news was difficult, the severance package that came with it was surprisingly generous. At least I had some financial cushion to soften the blow, and it set the stage for what I thought would be a new chapter filled with promise.

At that point, I was staying with my cousin Yolanda. Moving in with her seemed like the right move, given the circumstances. We began brainstorming the idea of starting a nonprofit organization together. I had been passionate about giving back to the community and even considered starting my own nonprofit to mentor young girls. The idea of helping Yolanda with a summer food program she had started felt like a perfect fit. With the money I had saved, along with my severance from ATI, I figured I could take a leap of faith and help her get her own venture really rolling. The concept and the contacts were already in place. She just needed me to help her get it off the ground.

Yolanda had always been a bit of a hustler. She had this knack for getting by, often through questionable means. Over the years, I had heard stories about her manipulative tendencies—how she could be a con artist if she wanted to be. Despite those warnings, I never believed she would turn that side of herself on me. We were family, after all. Family's different, right? In hindsight, I should have listened to the whispers and the red flags but at the time, I was eager to help her out.

She needed capital to get started, and I had a small nest egg that I was willing to invest. She convinced me that she had a solid plan for her summer food program and that the money would go toward renting vans to deliver meals to various sites. She needed $15,000, which I had readily available in my account. Additionally, since her credit was less than stellar, I agreed to put the rental vans in my name. It was supposed to be a temporary, short-term solution until the business started generating enough income to stand on its own. It was a risky move, but I wanted to believe in her and in what we could build together.

For a while, things seemed to go smoothly. She got a really large house, and I moved in with her and brought my son with me. TJ was 10 at the time and settled in comfortably, but the cracks began to show soon enough. Yolanda hadn't held up her end of the bargain. The business plans we had discussed remained just that—plans. She didn't follow through on the steps we had agreed upon for the nonprofit, and her own summer food program was floundering. Her life, always a bit chaotic, began to spill over into mine. The rental vans we had leased started showing signs of damage. Yolanda, in typical fashion, tried to handle it in the most underhanded way possible. Instead of returning the vans and reporting the damages, she hired someone to try and fix them without the rental company noticing. Of course, they did notice. The vans were returned in worse shape than before and the rental company came after me for tens of thousands of dollars in damages.

Suddenly, I found myself with a massive bill, a lien on my credit report, and no easy way out. Most of the money I had saved up was gone. I had given it all to Yolanda. The debt was mounting. I couldn't believe I had let myself get dragged into such a mess. It wasn't just the money that stung—it was the betrayal. Yolanda, the person I had trusted to help me, had not only failed to deliver on her promises but had left me to clean up the disaster she had created. The tension between us reached a boiling point, and we stopped speaking altogether. Living in the same house with her became unbearable. The air was thick with resentment and every day felt like I was walking on eggshells. I could no longer justify giving her the benefit of the doubt, nor could I keep letting her back into my life after each disappointment. She was messy in every sense of the word, and I was done letting her mess spill into my world.

I was mentally and emotionally exhausted. My finances were diminishing, and I didn't even have a job to fall back on. My son needed stability, and I needed a fresh start. Atlanta had been on my mind for a while, and even though I had resisted moving back for years—because of work, or TJ, or whatever excuse I could find—it started to feel like my only option. It wasn't an easy decision. I didn't want to move somewhere new without any safety net but staying in the same environment was slowly suffocating me. My son was reaching an age where he needed structure, and I couldn't keep subjecting him to the dysfunction that had taken root in our home with Yolanda. Going back to live with my Aunt Roz didn't feel like a real option either, not after everything I had been through.

In October 2011, my best friend, Sandy and I were walking and chatting. I told her I wanted to move back to Atlanta. Immediately she dove right in and helped me pack up my stuff and within two weeks I was driving away. The house that had once seemed like an opportunity was in my rearview mirror. Atlanta was ahead of me, offering a blank slate—a chance to start over, even if I didn't fully know what that looked like yet. I had no job lined up, no clear plan, but for the first time in a long while, I felt a sense of hope. I was leaving behind the mess, the disappointment, and the pain of being let down by someone I trusted. The road ahead was uncertain, but at least it was mine to navigate.

When I first moved back to Atlanta, I stayed with a friend to get my bearings. It was a strange time for me—everything felt like it was in flux. TJ stayed behind with his dad for a short while but as expected, that arrangement didn't last long. His dad, unfortunately, wasn't close to winning a Father of the Year award. It became clear that TJ needed to come back and live with me, and with that change, my priorities shifted dramatically.

I had started my first business, which was exciting, along with a nonprofit organization that I was passionate about. The nonprofit focused on helping young girls between the ages of 11 and 16 with their mental, spiritual, physical, and emotional well-being. I even ran free camps for them. It was fulfilling work, but it didn't pay the bills. Nonprofits rarely do. With my son moving back in, I had to face the reality of my financial situation. I needed a steady job. So I put my dreams of the nonprofit on the back burner and jumped back into the staffing industry. It wasn't what I had envisioned for myself, but it provided the stability I needed for TJ and me. Dating wasn't even on my radar. I was focused on getting my life in order, rediscovering who I was outside of all the chaos, and healing from my past relationships.

Taking a break from abusive relationships was like breathing fresh air for the first time. I realized that I hadn't loved myself for a long time, which is why I tolerated the abuse for as long as I did. That break gave me the space to learn what self-love really meant and the importance of setting boundaries—boundaries I had never enforced in my life before. It was during that period that I began to confront the things from my childhood that I had never dealt with. It became clear to me that the unresolved pain from my past was what had allowed me to accept mistreatment in my relationships. The sexual abuse that I experienced at an early age took me down a river that led me to accept the ocean of physical abuse I waded in as I grew older.

> *The abuse I had endured as an adult was just an extension of the emotional scars I carried from my earlier years.*

The pact of secrecy those predatorial, old men made me agree to is what led me to think it was acceptable to be the "other woman" in my relationships. Some of those relationships were with men who lied to me until I discovered the truth while others were with men who were honest with me about their other relationships from the beginning. The abuse I had endured as an adult was just an extension of the emotional scars I carried from my earlier years.

I realized I had been naive. I used to judge women who stayed in abusive relationships, thinking that I would never allow someone to treat me like that.

The truth is when you're broken, you accept things you never thought you would. My experience taught me that. I learned that the abuse I had tolerated wasn't just physical. It was emotional and mental long before it became physical. Getting out of that cycle of abuse forced me to confront my pain head-on. It was impossible to hide from it anymore. For a long time, I didn't feel proud of myself for leaving, but eventually, I began to realize how much strength it took. I now know that my son was one of the main reasons I was able to leave. I didn't want him to witness any form of abuse, and I knew it was only a matter of time before he would if I stayed. I left for him, just like I left Dallas and my father behind for him.

Leaving Dallas had been a difficult decision. My father had struggled with addiction for as long as I could remember, and I didn't want my son to be exposed to the things I had seen growing up. As a child, you don't always understand what's happening, but those memories stay with you, imprinted like a tattoo in your mind. I didn't want TJ to grow up with the same images burned into his memory, so I made the difficult choice to leave my dad and the toxic environment behind to build a better life for us in Atlanta.

But even as I was trying to rebuild my life in Atlanta, new challenges arose. Aunt Roz had always been like a mother to me so when she started to get sick, I was really concerned. I referred to her as my mother and she protected me like one of her own daughters. I lost my birth mother, my grandmother, and had to come to terms that I may be losing my other mother too. She had been acting very strange and we soon discovered she had dementia. That diagnosis turned my world upside down once again. My mom had always been the strong one, the one who held everything together. She needed help, and it became clear that someone needed to be with her full-time.

At the time, a distant cousin was living with my mother, but he had been there before she got sick. As her condition worsened, BeBe and I had to make some tough decisions. We both agreed we were going to keep her in her home for as long as possible. Neither one of us wanted to put her in a nursing home. Bebe and I got on a call and discussed the situation. Should the cousin stay with her, or should Yolanda move in to help? It was an intense conversation, and I found myself stuck in the middle. Bebe didn't want Yolanda to move in.

She was adamant that Yolanda would mishandle my mother's finances and not provide the care she needed. I thought differently. Despite my own personal experience running a business with Yolanda, I couldn't believe that Yolanda would take advantage of her own mother. In the end, I cast the deciding vote and Yolanda moved in.

At first, it seemed like the right decision. I visited often, and Yolanda appeared to be doing well taking care of our mother. But as time passed, things began to unravel. Every time I visited, my mother seemed worse as her dementia progressed faster than I had expected. I started hearing whispers that Yolanda wasn't there much, leaving the care of my mother to her teenage children. Still, I gave Yolanda the benefit of the doubt. It's not easy being a primary caretaker, especially when dealing with someone with dementia. I could imagine how exhausting and stressful it must have been. I tried to visit as often as I could to help relieve Yolanda and give her a break. One visit stands out in my mind. I arrived at the house and everything felt off. Yolanda wasn't there, as usual. Her middle child, Crystal, was in charge, and I could tell something wasn't right. I went to check on my mother and what I found still haunts me. She was lying in bed, soaked in urine—not from a single accident but from what looked like an entire day of neglect. The house was a mess with empty fast food bags all over the place, dirty dishes piled a mile high in the sink. I couldn't even find basic necessities like soap or clean clothes for her. I was furious.

I confronted Yolanda immediately and of course, she had an excuse. She claimed it wasn't as bad as it looked, that she was doing the best she could. By then, I knew better. Yolanda wasn't staying with my mother anymore. She had gotten her own apartment, leaving her children and random strangers to take care of a woman who had worked hard her entire life and deserved much better than this neglect. Yolanda was an opportunist and would take advantage of ANYONE who crossed her path, even her own mother. My mother had worked for AT&T for 40 years, bought her house outright, and paid cash for a new car. She had the resources to be cared for properly and yet there she was, being treated like an afterthought.

I knew I had to do something. I started making moves to gain custody of my mother. Bebe was on board, and even Yolanda's oldest daughter, Valencia, offered to support me in getting her the help she deserved. But Yolanda wasn't happy about it. The situation became even more hostile. When I came to visit, her children were instructed not to let me in. I remember standing on the porch, knocking and calling out, desperate to check on my mom. It was heartbreaking. Through it all, I had to keep pushing forward. I still had my own life to manage, my son to care for, and my job to maintain. The situation with my mom was consuming, but I refused to give up. The experience showed me just how complicated family dynamics can be, especially when illness and money are involved. It also taught me that even in the face of family betrayal and dysfunction, I had to stand up for what was right, no matter how difficult it was. It soon came at a cost.

PURPOSE NOTE

This chapter delves into the emotional and psychological ties that can bind us to toxic relationships, even within our own family. My relationship with Sharonda reflected the unresolved abandonment issues I carried for years. While it wasn't the physical abuse I had endured in the past, the emotional manipulation and betrayal were a continuation of the patterns I'd lived through before. I stayed too long not because of loyalty, but because those old wounds— feeling abandoned and searching for connection—kept me stuck.

Leaving Yolanda felt like another significant loss, though it wasn't marked by death. It was the painful realization that I had once again been holding on to a relationship where I was needed but not truly wanted. This became clear as I saw how my role was more about what I could provide rather than being valued for who I was. I wasn't just walking away from her but from another form of emotional abuse that I hadn't recognized earlier.

Deciding to leave was an act of courage, forcing me to break the cycle. Like many times before, when the need for change hit me, I moved quickly. Atlanta became my escape once again—a place where I could reset, distance myself from the dysfunction, and reclaim a sense of self. Moving swiftly has always been how I handled these moments of clarity, where the need to protect myself and my son became the priority.

This chapter taught me that it's not just romantic relationships that can be toxic. Sometimes it's family too. I learned that being needed is not the same as being wanted or valued. Walking away from Yolanda wasn't just about cutting ties with her. It was about ending the emotional hold that my past abandonment had over me and learning that I deserve more than to simply be tolerated.

8

Ready or Not

Was I ready for love?
SHERMIE HARGROVE

I met my husband Lionel at Bahama Breeze, a laid-back, island-themed restaurant in Atlanta. It was a regular night out with friends, nothing too special. My girlfriend Kanetra had flown in from Dallas and Natalie, my other friend who lived in town, joined us as well. We were sitting at the bar, catching up and enjoying each other's company while several different men approached us through the night and tried to keep us company. Lionel noticed me sitting there as well. I hadn't paid him any attention at the time but looking back, I realize he had his eyes on me from the moment I walked in.

Kanetra and I eventually left the bar, planning to head home. We found ourselves in the parking lot chatting with a group of guys standing next to their car, which just so happened to be parked in front of ours. Natalie was striking up a conversation with one of the guys and before I knew it, Lionel walked over and introduced himself.

At first, we engaged in light banter. He started talking about fitness, more specifically LA Fitness, and we found ourselves in a playful debate over which location was better. We laughed about the one where everybody goes to be seen and how we never see anyone sweat in that location. They were too busy trying to be cute. There was something about the ease of our conversation, the way he made me laugh without even trying. By the end of our exchange, he asked for my number and boldly inquired if he could take me out to breakfast the following day, which happened to be a Sunday.

Right to the point, I thought. I kind of liked that. But Sundays are my sacred days—my time to unwind, reflect, and prepare for the week ahead. Plus, I had to drop Kanetra off at the airport in the morning. I wasn't feeling the idea of a first date, but Kanetra nudged me, encouraging me to give it a shot. Lionel persisted, suggesting that we meet after I dropped Kanetra off at the airport. I still wasn't sure, but something about his laid-back charm had me saying, "Okay, I'll think about it."

The next day came, and as I dropped Kanetra off, Lionel called. "Hey! What's up?" He sounded genuinely excited to meet up. "What time did we say we were meeting?"

I tried to come up with an excuse and said, "Well, hello, but I never said we were meeting. It's Sunday. I just dropped my friend off at the airport. I'm not dressed..."

He cut me off. "As long as your hair looks as good as it did yesterday, I don't care what you wear!"

I worked hard at maintaining my hair, so I really appreciated the comment.

"So what's up? Are we still on for brunch?"

After a little internal debate, I replied, "Why not?"

I agreed to meet him at Mimi's Café for brunch. The spot was cozy and inviting. From the moment we sat down, the conversation flowed effortlessly. We spent hours talking about everything—our pasts, our dreams, our families. At the end of the date, he asked if he could see me the next day, and then the day after that. And so it began. Lionel worked a late shift and then from 1 p.m. to 10 p.m. and every other weekend, but he still made time for us. I appreciated that effort more than I realized at the time. He was intentional about everything, especially about me, which stood out.

Lionel had two sons, ages 8 and 11. My son, TJ, was about the same age as his oldest, and one day they all met at the park. It was natural, like they'd known each other forever. The boys got along great, and it was as if everything was falling into place. But while our relationship blossomed, Lionel was quietly dealing with some significant challenges. He had recently discovered he had a daughter from a previous relationship, and the child's mother had put him on child support. At the time, his daughter was two. The weight of the news, combined with the fact that he was underemployed at the time, was starting to take a toll on him. He didn't let it show, though. I admired how despite everything he was going through, he still made me and our relationship a priority.

Things moved quickly between us. Lionel's financial situation had become dire. He was about to lose his home. We decided that he would move in with me after he short-sold his house. It felt right at the time but little did I know my own insecurities were about to surface in ways I hadn't anticipated.

Lionel wasn't always the best at returning calls or being entirely honest about things. There was this one incident where I went through his phone and a woman–supposedly just a friend of his–had sent him some half-naked photos wearing a bra and panties with a text that read, "What do you think?" I texted back, "I think you should be sending this to someone else!" I confronted him about it and naturally, we had a blowout fight. I even packed up his belongings from my place and told him to come get them before I threw them out. He came, collected his stuff, and left. That was the first real bump in the road for us.

Looking back, I realize I was operating from a place of unhealed wounds. I had trauma I hadn't dealt with, and it was spilling over into my relationship with Lionel. After that episode, Lionel decided he wasn't ready to move in with me. Instead, he moved in with a roommate. While we continued dating, things weren't the same. Our relationship became increasingly rocky. Lionel's moods were unpredictable, and I found myself catching him in little lies more and more frequently. One night, he wasn't answering several of my calls. When he did finally answer, he said he was watching the game and couldn't talk long. Something didn't sit right with me. I've been told a woman should always trust her tuition and since he lived right around the corner, I decided to drive over to his place. I pulled up to find him outside, walking around with another woman. I lost it. I had just thrown the flowers he'd recently given me at him, creating a dramatic scene right there in the parking lot.

Around this time, I was preparing for a trip to New York with a group of girl-friends and a few guy friends. I was emotionally drained from everything going on with Lionel, so the getaway couldn't have come at a better time. During the trip, I met a guy named Brian, who was friends with one of the girls in our group. He was charming, and he was coming on to me strongly! It would have been easy to let my guard down, but I stayed loyal to Lionel, even though our relationship was hanging on by a thread. I told Brian I was in a relationship back home and the only thing we could do was be friends. When I returned from New York, Lionel wasn't any different. In fact, he seemed even more distant. He had cooked dinner one night and when I asked if I could have some, he snapped at me.

"Why are you asking me a stupid question? What am I going to say? No?"

It was something so small but in that moment, it felt like the last straw. A week earlier I had a guy coming on to me who was ready to take me on trips around the world, but I had to deal with this at home? Deep down, I think I was looking for a reason to end things and Lionel gave me just that. We broke up in September of 2012. It was a painful split, but it was necessary. The love we had for each other wasn't enough to overcome the issues we both carried into the relationship. I was still healing, and Lionel had his own battles to fight. Despite how things ended, I don't regret our time together. Lionel showed me what it felt like to be pursued with intention, and for that, I'm grateful.

> *The love we had for each other wasn't enough to overcome the issues we both carried into the relationship.*

After Lionel and I broke up, it didn't take long for me to reconnect with Brian. He was a nice enough guy, someone I could spend time with and take my mind off the mess I had just gone through with Lionel. He wasn't perfect but then again, neither was I. I was still carrying all of the emotional baggage from my breakup, and it felt good to have someone there, even if it was a temporary dis-traction. After Lionel and I called it quits, Brian came up from Miami to spend some time with me.

It wasn't long before fate decided to play its little game of irony. One Wednesday, of all days, we ran into Lionel at a spot we frequented. Nobody went to this place on a Wednesday, especially not Lionel. You can imagine my surprise when we walked in and there he was. It was awkward, to say the least. Lionel gave me this look like he couldn't believe I had already moved on. I could see the judgment in his eyes, though he didn't say much at the moment. But I knew I wasn't off the hook just yet. Later, Brian also had something to say about the whole run-in. He felt like I had put him in an uncomfortable situation, almost like it wasn't completely over between Lionel and me. To be fair, Brian wasn't entirely wrong. My feelings for Lionel were complicated, even though we were technically done. I could sense that Brian wasn't thrilled about the idea of dating someone who still had unresolved feelings for her ex. We tried to push through and keep things going, despite the awkwardness.

Shortly after, I took a trip to Miami. Brian and I were still dating, or at least trying to. During that trip, things began to unravel between us. I found out that Brian had been lying to me about a few things. It wasn't anything huge at first, just little white lies, but as they say, "What's done in the dark eventually comes to light." Turns out, Brian had some girls he was keeping on the side. He thought I would be okay with it. Once I realized Brian wasn't any different from the men I'd tried to distance myself from, I cut things off with him.

Life has a funny way of bringing people back into your orbit, even when you think you're done with them. Fast forward a bit, and I ran into Lionel again. This time, it was at a wing joint we both liked, right next to his barbershop. I had been heading there for some food and sure enough, Lionel was at the barbershop with his boys. As I walked in, we locked eyes, and it was like we had both been caught off guard. He came over, smiling, and we exchanged a few awkward pleasantries.

"My God," Lionel said, laughing a little, "I was just talking about you."

I wasn't in the mood for small talk. My wisdom teeth were acting up, and I had an appointment to get them removed in the next couple of days so I was short with him.

"Yeah, well, my tooth hurts. I'm not gonna stand out here and talk. If you wanna catch up, call me later," I told him, not expecting much to come from it.

Later that evening, he did call and to my surprise, he offered to take me to my dentist appointment. "Who's taking you to get your wisdom teeth out?" he asked.

"I have it covered," I replied vaguely, but Lionel wasn't one to let things go easily.

"I'll take off work," he insisted. "I want to take care of you."

That was Lionel for you. He had this way of slipping back into my life just when I thought I was ready to move on. So he took me to the dentist and from there, we started talking more regularly again. We eased back into a relationship, although things weren't exactly smooth. Lionel's work schedule was hectic, and his personality could be unpredictable. He was on edge most of the time, and I didn't deal with it head-on because I had grown used to brushing things under the rug.

For the first two-and-a-half years, Lionel and I didn't live together. I had always said I wouldn't give a man more than two years to figure out if he wanted to spend the rest of his life with me. In my mind, if a man didn't know by then, he probably wasn't ever going to know, and I wasn't about to waste more time than that. Lionel must have remembered that because just two years and four months into our relationship, he proposed—on my birthday, no less.

I kind of knew it was coming. We had already gone ring shopping, and I had a feeling he was going to pop the question on my birthday. Still, the moment was special, and I appreciated the effort he put into making it memorable. That was one of the things I always admired about Lionel. He had a way of making even the smallest gestures feel grand. So we got engaged and after two years of engagement, we got married. The truth was, deep down, I knew things weren't perfect between us. We had different views on life, love, and especially parenting. The way we were raised was night and day—his parents had been together for over 50 years, while I came from a broken home. He had not yet experienced the loss of a loved one while I had lost several people close to me. Those differences started to show more as time went on.

The real cracks in our relationship began to form when Lionel lost his job a year before our wedding. He was unemployed for nine months, and even though he had a transportation business, it wasn't enough to make ends meet.

He wasn't contributing much financially, and I could see the toll it was taking on his self-esteem. He became distant, moody, and harder to talk to. Lionel blamed his behavior on the stress of being unemployed, but it didn't make things any easier for me. Eventually, he found a job in his field, and for a moment, it felt like we were turning a corner. He was happier, more present, and I dared to believe we were finally building the life we had promised each other.

Just three months into his new job, my world shattered. I discovered he was having an affair with a coworker. We had only been married for six months. Six months, and already I was facing the harsh reality of his betrayal. The pain was unbearable, like a shock to the heart, but worse than that was the growing feeling that I wasn't enough. I had stood by him through his financial difficulties. I made him feel like a man when he couldn't provide, and yet here I was, cast aside for someone else. I began to wonder if maybe I was the one who wasn't worth fighting for, if somehow this was my fault. The man I'd known wasn't right for me had confronted my deepest fear that I wasn't deserving of loyalty or real love.

> *The man I'd known wasn't right for me had confronted my deepest fear that I wasn't deserving of loyalty or real love.*

But that wasn't the only issue we were facing. Lionel had two kids from his previous marriage and while I initially got along well with his ex-wife, Tammy, things took a turn when her relationships started to fail. In the 12 years Lionel and I were together, Tammy had four different fiancés. Each time one relationship ended, she became more of a problem in our lives. When she had a man in her life, everything was fine. We could co-parent smoothly without issues. But when she was single, it was like she wanted to control everything, including Lionel. At first, I would express my concerns to Lionel about the way he and Tammy communicated. They didn't have babies anymore, their kids were teenagers. There was no reason for them to be talking about every little thing. I used to ask him, "Why is she so worried about what we got going on over here?" I also used to ask him, "How does she know about what's going on over here?" But my concerns always fell on deaf ears. Lionel dismissed my feelings and eventually, I stopped bringing them up. I tried to ignore it, thinking it would go away on its own but of course, it didn't.

The final blow came during Christmas. We were at Tammy's house, having Christmas dinner with her family. I wasn't around when it started, but Lionel and Tammy got into a heated argument. Then for some reason, Lionel started arguing with Tammy's sister, and it turned into a huge scene. I was embarrassed, but it was just another episode in the long list of conflicts between them.

Things came to a head when Lionel and Tammy's latest fiancé, James, started having problems. James didn't like Lionel, and Lionel didn't like James. It was a mess. On Father's Day, Lionel went over to their house to confront James about some things he had heard. I didn't even know Lionel had gone over there, but James had my email from a previous interaction and let me know about the altercation. I was furious. Why was Lionel going over there and causing drama? I had told him time and time again that he needed to set boundaries with Tammy, but he never listened. I kept thinking to myself, "Why is Tammy telling James what Lionel says about him, and why is Lionel telling Tammy how he feels about James?" I made a comment to James saying if Tammy is going to keep feeding the fish, the fish are going to keep eating. It got back to her and she didn't like it.

Previously I had hired Tammy to make a custom suit for my son. He needed it for a presentation at this program he had been accepted into at Yale University. I contacted her to check on her progress, but she never responded. Later I found out that she had no intention of finishing my son's suit and was calling him a drug addict!

"You can't force me to do shit," she said.

"Bitch, please. I already paid you," I responded.

She took exception to me calling her a bitch, but I had no idea she had so much ammunition to fire back on me. She knew way too much about me. She knew about my abusive relationship. She knew about my dead mother. Mind you, Lionel was part of our text exchange and didn't say a word. I was so pissed because I knew she could only know those things through Lionel. The next thing I know, I'm in a car with my girlfriend, headed to a park ready to beat some ass! Fortunately, cooler heads prevailed and we never met up.

The situation with Lionel's ex-wife and his constant failure to stand up for me made it clear that our marriage was doomed. We tried to make it work, but the damage was done. Their son Brandon had been living with us for almost a year because he didn't get along with his mother's fiancé. Tammy thought he'd be better off with his dad in his life on a daily basis as he transitioned into his early teenage years. I was completely on board with the idea and got along great with Brandon, however, one day while Lionel and I were at work, Tammy moved Brandon out of the house without telling us. There was just too much drama going on for me. I began to emotionally check out of the marriage and eventually, I began to seek comfort elsewhere and began to get emotionally involved with another gentleman who lived in Miami. There was no real excuse for what I did but I felt lost, disconnected, and completely disillusioned with my marriage.

By the time Lionel and I finally separated, it was long overdue. We were living separate lives, just going through the motions. We had tried therapy, but Lionel refused to take it seriously. I made the decision to move out, and we officially ended things in November of 2019. Looking back, I realize that Lionel and I were never truly compatible. Our differences were too great, and we both carried too much unresolved pain into the relationship.

PURPOSE NOTE

This chapter is a reflection of love, loss, and the lessons learned through relationships that were meant to teach, not last. My relationship with Lionel was a significant turning point, revealing the importance of addressing personal wounds before entering into deep commitments. His pursuit of me with intention initially felt like everything I had wanted, but it also highlighted the unhealed parts of myself that I had not yet faced.

The emotional rollercoaster of our relationship—with its highs of love and connection and lows of betrayal and unresolved issues—taught me that love alone is not enough to sustain a relationship. It's not enough if the trust is broken or if past traumas are left unresolved. While I stayed loyal, even when faced with temptation, the underlying cracks in our foundation kept widening.

This relationship also showed me how vital boundaries are, not only with our partners but with the people they bring into their lives. The constant entanglement with Lionel's ex-wife, his failure to protect me, and my frustration with being caught in their unresolved drama revealed that I deserve to be in a relationship where I am prioritized and respected.

Through it all, I learned that staying in a relationship to avoid loneliness or out of fear of abandonment only leads to more pain. Walking away was hard, but it became clear that choosing myself and my own healing was the most loving thing I could do. This chapter is a reminder that we cannot fix what is broken in others, nor can we be the solution to someone else's unresolved struggles. True love starts with healing ourselves first, and it's only then that we can attract and build the kind of love we truly deserve.

9

I Choose Me

The best decision I ever made
SHERMIE HARGROVE

During my separation, I found myself drawn back to familiarity, craving connection without the expectation of anything serious. Casey was my "oldie but goodie," someone I'd always felt a connection with, yet neither of us wanted more. Only seeing each other when I went to Dallas, it felt safe and uncomplicated; we both knew what to expect, and it was comfortable.

Then, I reconnected with one of the guys that was on the trip in New York, who brought an unexpected emotional connection. He offered a kind of understanding I hadn't realized I was missing. Our connection deepened naturally, and throughout the separation, he provided a sense of being seen and understood when I needed it most.

None of this was happening locally. It was as if I had constructed boundaries around myself—stepping out only when I was far enough away. Lionel and I were separated at the time and found ourselves in this never-ending cycle of not getting along. The whole situation stressed me out and I needed a release. We had separated right at the end of our lease. I moved into my own place in November 2019. We didn't see each other for a while after that, but there were conditions if we were ever to get back together. One of them was therapy and predictably, Lionel refused. I continued my therapy, trying to find my footing. In the meantime, my mistake was agreeing to continue seeing him and spending time with him while I figured it all out.

Then COVID came, and we ended up quarantined together. I thought it would only last a couple of weeks, but then the entire world shut down. The next thing I knew, we were living together again. Lionel was temporarily staying with a friend and hadn't gotten his own place yet, so that worked out perfectly. He started spending more time with me and unexpectedly, things between us began to improve. I cut off every relationship I had during our separation. We got creative and found ways to enjoy each other's company again, but life is never that straightforward.

Hearing the word was like a bomb going off, leaving my ears ringing. My best cousin, Tannah, called to deliver the news: my father, who was living in Dallas at the time, had been diagnosed with cancer. That terrible word came with a prognosis—a rough estimate of six months to a year, but somebody lied. It was surreal. Everything seemed to move in slow motion as I processed the reality. I knew I had to bring him home with me to take care of him, so I made plans to pick him up. But it didn't play out as expected. My father's condition worsened much faster than the doctors had anticipated.

Before my father was placed in hospice care, I took him around the neighborhood for some ice cream. I pushed him around in his wheelchair, being he could not walk at the time. The ice cream shop wasn't far, and it was a gesture I knew would lift his spirits. He smiled weakly as he licked his cone, a little glimmer in his eyes. Later, as he lay in bed growing weaker each day, he asked me to stay close. He never wanted me far from his side but instead in the room with him just so he could see my face. I felt like he wanted me to know that I was one of the things in his life he felt he had gotten right. I was Dad's comfort in his time of need, his reminder that despite everything, he had done something good when he had me.

> *I was Dad's comfort in his time of need, his reminder that despite everything, he had done something good when he had me.*

I watched, helplessly, as life drained from his body day by day. It was as if a part of me was fading along with him. I didn't realize just how much of a toll it was taking on me until I found myself still grieving long after he passed. I thought I was holding it together for everyone else but the strain crept up on me, slowly squeezing my heart until it felt like I couldn't breathe. During that time, Lionel wasn't the most compassionate person to be around. Our relationship had always been tumultuous, but the stress of watching my father die combined with Lionel's lack of understanding made everything so much worse.

One evening, we ended up in a heated argument over something trivial. I don't even remember what it was about. I had just recovered from a stint of COVID, which meant I had been forced to stay away from my father for 11 days. It was agonizing to be so close yet unable to see him, knowing he was suffering and I couldn't comfort him. But I couldn't risk exposing him to the virus in his fragile state. Finally, when I was allowed to be around him again, I noticed he was shivering all the time. He had lost so much weight he was down to 94 pounds. He was always cold, lying under an air vent in his room. I asked Lionel to help me rearrange things to make my father more comfortable. I tried to keep my distance to be cautious, but it was hard. Lionel was being his typical self—harsh, curt, and condescending.

"No, don't move it there. Put it over HERE!" he barked.

The last thing I wanted was for my dad to feel like he was an inconvenience in his own home. I tried to tell Lionel to chill out, but he snapped at me. There's no way he would have talked that way to me in front of my daddy if he wasn't sick. My father would have stepped into him! But I had to fight for myself. The argument escalated and before I knew it, I was hysterically crying. I couldn't catch my breath, probably because of the lingering effects of COVID, or maybe just from the overwhelming stress and sadness.

That night, I woke up in the middle of the night with my chest tightening and my right side feeling numb. It felt like my body was betraying me. Was I dying? Was this COVID or something worse? I dialed 911, convinced I might not make it. Lionel, who wasn't even sleeping in the same room as me, remained distant and unbothered, lounging on the couch. As I waited for the ambulance to arrive, I called my son, TJ. I needed to hear his voice. I needed

> *I needed to feel connected to something that wasn't pain and fear. If this was the end for me, I wanted my son's voice to be the last thing I heard.*

to feel connected to something that wasn't pain and fear. If this was the end for me, I wanted my son's voice to be the last thing I heard.

When the paramedics arrived, they checked my vitals. My blood pressure was through the roof—194 over something. They said they didn't think it was COVID. Instead, they suspected a severe anxiety attack. They tried to calm me down, gently encouraging me to get out of my head. My dad, miraculously, slept through the commotion. The next morning, as if nothing had happened, Lionel and I had another spat. I was selling my son's old car to a friend of mine. Lionel called himself helping me out and taking charge, but I just wanted to get rid of the car. It wasn't a big deal to me, and I was selling it to someone I knew. Would you believe he started yelling, cursing, and berating me over something insignificant while I was still reeling from what had happened the night before? It was like he couldn't—or wouldn't—see that I was hanging on by a thread.

"You always think you know every fucking thing! Sick of this shit." he exclaimed, making it clear he didn't give a damn about me.

We were supposed to close on a new house that I'd hoped would make my father more comfortable in his final days. We had put down several thousand dollars and were set to move in on July 25. It was two weeks before the move and I was having serious doubts about whether I wanted to be with Lionel at all. I started looking for ways to get out of the commitment. Could I pull out of the deal? Could I find a new place? Everything felt overwhelming, and I thought maybe God was telling me to just keep moving forward despite everything.

The day of the closing arrived, and Lionel and I got into another terrible argument. I don't even know what set it off. I told him to take me back home. I do remember us tossing water on each other-it was a mess! When we got back, my aunt, who was caring for my father, told me I needed a break. She insisted I go somewhere and find some peace. Later, I went up to the rooftop pool with a friend to clear my head. I never get in pools because of my hair but that night,

I submerged myself completely. It was a brief, rare moment of serenity. When I got back, my dad was lying in bed, a shell of the man he once was. Then the strangest thing happened. My dad started pouring water all over himself.

"Stop that, Daddy! Why are you pouring water all over yourself?" I asked, wondering if he could tell I had been to the pool.

Next, my aunt and I watched my father as a gospel song played gently in the background. It was a deeply emotional moment. Was he baptizing himself, preparing for the end? For the first time, I broke down completely in front of him. I had tried to be so strong, holding everything together, but he saw me crumble that night. Exhausted, I went to sleep. Lionel offered to watch over my dad so I could get some rest. It was around 5 a.m. when I woke up to Lionel calling my name. My father had fallen out of bed again. I rushed into the room, but when I saw him, I knew he was gone.

"He's dead," I said, the words falling out of my mouth like stones. The reality hit me hard and fast. My father died the day after we closed on the house. The timing felt like a cruel joke.

I missed a call from him that night and found a text from him that simply said, "Please help me." I'll never know what he was trying to tell me in those final moments, but I have to live with the fact that I wasn't there. My father's mind was still sharp until the very end, but his body had given out. Even in his last days, he had texted Lionel, reminding him to carry me over the threshold of our new home. I lost my father that day, and I lost a part of myself too.

Masked up and spaced out, we gathered at a local park in honor of my father and released doves, symbolizing his spirit being set free. The small gathering, though limited in size by the circumstances, was rich in emotion. Despite his challenges, it was evident that my father was loved. We all retreated to a rooftop for an intimate memorial, the city skyline standing witness as we shared stories, offered prayers, and found solace in each other's presence despite the distance that the pandemic had imposed on us.

I learned to press forward, even when the weight of my experiences threatened to hold me back. When Lionel and I moved into the new house, I hoped for a fresh start, some semblance of stability and maybe even a way to heal. I cut off all ties to relationships I created during our separation. I wanted us to work. He would be my new support system, after all, my dad was gone and the only immediate family left in my life was my son. But the change of scenery couldn't mask the disconnect that had formed between us. Lionel was still up to his old ways and was cheating on me. One night as we were lying in bed, I saw the light of his phone. He was texting his mistress in the bed right next to me. Catching him in the act was a clear indication that they were still involved and once again, I felt betrayed.

Not long after, my son moved in too, adding a new dynamic to an already strained environment. I had noticed some character flaws that I needed to check him on before he entered adulthood. Then one of Lionel's sons came to stay with us. I began to see Lionel's true character more clearly and although I'd said it before, it wasn't a reflection I could ignore any longer.

That was the year everything shifted. It was during that time we learned that Lionel's youngest son was gay. Lionel couldn't accept it, and his mom wouldn't accept it either. They both thought he was going through a phase and he would outgrow his "gayness." When that didn't work, they enrolled him in military school, thinking that would somehow "straighten" him up. But there was no amount of PT and drill that could change who he was. So his mother, in all her rigid intolerance, told him he had only two choices: Either return to military school or find someplace else to live. Either way, she made it clear he wasn't welcome in her home. At that time, Lionel and I weren't even in regular contact with his son, Brandon. He and I hadn't spoken in years, not since his mother moved him out of our home.

I didn't know what to expect when Brandon came back into the picture. It had been two years since I'd seen or talked to him. He was a teenager trying to figure out who he was in the world. When he finally moved in with Lionel and me, something unexpected happened. I thought it'd be awkward and tense but instead, Brandon gravitated toward me. Maybe he could see I was there to protect him, to give him space to be who he was—something his own father refused to do. Lionel was still stuck in this denial, pretending not to notice his son's sexuality, turning a blind eye like it was all some misunderstanding. He truly believed if a tree falls in the forest and no one is around to hear it, it doesn't make a sound. But Brandon saw that I accepted him, no conditions attached. It took a couple of months, but Brandon finally came out to me. It was his senior year in high school. He started talking, and I listened. He asked if I knew. I told him, "I had an idea, but it's not my place to put that label on you. You get to tell me who you are."

Meanwhile, my relationship with Lionel continued to unravel. Seeing how he treated Brandon just tore me apart. It made me question who I was, what I stood for, and whether I could even stand by this man who at his core wasn't the person I wanted to be with. If he couldn't love his son unconditionally, surely he couldn't love me unconditionally. I pulled back. My love and respect for him shrank day by day. Eventually, I decided I couldn't stay in a house with someone I no longer recognized. I didn't know who he was anymore, and I didn't even know what was going on in his life. He had received a job offer for a new position from a new employer that I didn't even know he had interviewed for. That's how far apart we had drifted.

I'd reached a breaking point. I asked Lionel for a divorce. It wasn't a decision I made lightly, and I felt a sense of obligation to keep things as steady as possible for Brandon. I promised Brandon that I wouldn't leave him until he graduated and headed off to college, and I meant to keep that promise. Initially, I planned to wait until Brandon graduated to tell Lionel, but things didn't work out that way. Lionel's constant needling and the incessant tension between us made it impossible to wait any longer. He knew by May. Still, I wasn't ready to walk away without ensuring that I was making the right decision. In June, I went to Mexico for 30 days, immersing myself in therapy three times a week. I confronted my emotions, dug deep, and ultimately arrived at the same conclusion: I wanted out. The distance solidified what I already knew—I needed to leave.

When I returned home in July, Lionel seemed to sense my resolve. He was ready to pay the entire mortgage, no more going half on it. He even finally agreed to start therapy. Then out of the blue, he proposed again, upgrading my ring in an attempt to reclaim something he must've known was lost. I couldn't say yes, though. I just didn't have it in me. Instead, I told him I needed to think about it, not because I had any doubts, but because I wanted to see if there was any possibility left, even just a sliver. Maybe if we went to counseling, maybe if we both tried. But deep down, I already knew the answer.

We started attending sessions, but the truth always finds a way to surface. One day, the therapist asked us point-blank: "Are you looking to save this or end it?" I had to be honest with the therapist, with Lionel, and most importantly, with myself. "I want to end it," I said, and there it was, out in the open.

While all of this was happening, Lionel's health began to decline. He'd been struggling with prostate issues, and the situation worsened throughout July. By August, just as I was ready to make my final decision, Lionel was diagnosed with bladder cancer. The cancer was aggressive, and it had already invaded the muscular layer of his bladder. He needed surgery, and fast. The procedure was scheduled for early September.

It felt like the universe was throwing one last curveball at me. I'd already decided to leave but was faced with a choice—stay and support him through this or walk away as planned. I chose to stay, at least for a while. Despite everything, I was still his wife, and I wasn't heartless. I even took him on a trip to New Orleans, one of his favorite cities, before his surgery. I could compartmentalize my feelings, put on a brave face, and act "wifey" but I knew deep down that I wasn't going to be able to do it forever.

The surgery on September 8 was grueling. Lionel was supposed to be in the hospital for a week, but complications arose and he ended up staying for 16 days. When he was finally discharged, we hoped the worst was behind us but an infection set in. We were back in the hospital for another two weeks. The man who had always prided himself on his physical strength now faced a reality where his body betrayed him daily. He had to wear a bag to catch his urine for the rest of his life, and the mental toll was immense.

There I was, caught between loyalty and self-preservation. How do you tell someone who's just gone through cancer surgery that you still want a divorce? I felt trapped. I had confided in his sister, who understood my situation, and I was grateful that someone in the family knew this wasn't a decision I made lightly. But telling Lionel outright still felt like an insurmountable task.

> *There I was, caught between loyalty and self-preservation.*

One night I sat on the cold shower floor, water cascading over me as I cried and wrapped myself up into a ball, filled with grief, guilt, and confusion. For an hour, I cried uncontrollably, my hands trembling as I prayed, begging for insight and the strength to leave Lionel. He had been trying to change, promising to be better but deep down, I felt the weight of years of pain. I was unable to shake the fear that it was too late. As the steam rose around me, I begged for clarity, torn between hope and the need to save myself.

In October, I had a trip planned to Dubai. It was supposed to be a getaway to clear my head, a break I'd desperately needed long before cancer became a part of our lives. I was torn. Do I go? Do I stay? With his mother's help, Lionel seemed stable enough and we'd communicated to the family that I was considering moving forward with the divorce. But disappointment and resentment hung in the air like chemtrails. Even as I boarded the plane, I knew I'd have to face it all when I returned. When I got back from Dubai, Lionel and I had another conversation. I told him that once I left for Africa in December—a trip I'd planned long ago with my son—I wasn't coming back to the house. We needed to put it up for sale and start disentangling our lives. It felt surreal to be planning a future without him while still living under the same roof, but I couldn't back down.

Through all of this, I realized I'd let so many boundaries slip over the years. When Lionel cheated, I'd told myself that was a line he couldn't cross. Instead of holding him accountable, I buried my feelings, letting resentment fester until I found myself doing things I never thought I would—like stepping out of my marriage. I justified it by telling myself that if he could betray me, I didn't owe him loyalty. But it wasn't me, and the dissonance tore me apart inside.

As time passed, I understood that I'd become skilled at distracting myself from pain rather than confronting it head-on. Losing my father, dealing with Lionel's betrayal, and then facing a divorce left me feeling that I wouldn't get a break in my life. I stayed busy, kept moving forward, but I never truly processed what I felt. It took therapy for me to realize how much I'd abandoned my own feelings.

PURPOSE NOTE

In the midst of navigating the complexities of my separation from Lionel, I found myself reckoning with loss and hard truths. The loss of my father, my last immediate relative, was a profound blow. His passing left me feeling untethered, as though a part of my identity was slipping away with him. Losing him while confronting the dissolution of my marriage created an emotional storm I hadn't been prepared for.

At the same time, facing Lionel's denial of his son's identity became a mirror for the deeper issues between us. His inability to love his son unconditionally revealed to me how he struggled to fully love me, too. It was in this moment of clarity that I realized how distant we were—emotionally and morally. Lionel's failure to embrace his son's truth showed me that I could no longer align myself with someone who lacked the capacity for unconditional love.

Throughout this chapter of my life, I was also forced to confront something I'd never really done before—choosing me. For so long, I had placed the needs of others above my own, letting my fear of being alone drive my decisions. But this time was different. I had to choose myself, or I felt I would die from the weight of the pain and the compromises I had been making. It wasn't just about surviving anymore. It was about living, fully and authentically, on my own terms. In choosing myself, I finally began to understand what it meant to heal and to honor my own worth.

10

Purpose Revealed

The reason why
SHERMIE HARGROVE

When I think of the only mother I ever really knew, Aunt Roz, I have a better understanding of how my marriage got off to a rocky start. She affected my marriage almost from the very beginning, but not in the ways you may think. Mom was never a meddler or monster-in-law. In fact, there was no way to tell if she even liked Lionel or not due to her mental issues and physical condition. I had barely settled into married life when I found myself losing my mother. It was such a tumultuous period, fraught with complications and emotional strain. I was still embroiled in a legal battle with Yolanda to secure custody, pouring all my energy and resources into that when suddenly my mother fell gravely ill. The timing was brutal.

I remember the day vividly. My husband and I were packing our bags for our first anniversary trip to New Orleans—a celebration meant to signify our new life together. I never would have thought that New Orleans would also signify the end of our life together as well. Just as I was putting the final touches on our itinerary, my cousin Valencia called, her voice tense, indicating that something was wrong.

"Grandma's in the hospital," she told me. "They're saying she's got two days left. You need to get here, now!"

I felt like Mike Tyson just hit me in my chest. It brought me to my knees, but that was okay. It made it easier to pray. In that instant, the world I had been desperately trying to hold together started crumbling at my feet. I immediately canceled our trip to New Orleans and booked a flight back to Texas. As much as I tried to prepare myself for what was waiting, nothing could have readied me for what I encountered.

When I walked into my childhood home, I was stunned. Yolanda—my estranged cousin and newfound nemesis—had moved back in. There was a stranger in my house. The house looked the same, but it felt completely foreign, like an illusion of what it once was. I noticed right away that my mother was no longer in her own bedroom. Yolanda had moved her into a cramped, poorly ventilated office space and taken over the master bedroom for herself. It was as if she had rearranged the entire house to erase any semblance of comfort and familiarity for my mother.

My mother's condition shocked me. She looked neglected and disheveled. Her once-bright eyes were clouded. Her mouth was dry and her gums were dark, making it look like her teeth were hurting her. Her hair was matted and dry, and her skin seemed dull. Her toenails were so overgrown it looked like they hadn't been clipped in weeks. I was appalled. This was not how you cared for someone in their final days.

I spent most of my time by her side, feeding her small bites of food, gently massaging her hands, and simply lying next to her. I spoke to her softly, even though she struggled to respond. I washed her hair, which was caked with dandruff, and combed through it until it shone again, imagining I could bring back a little of the dignity and grace she had always carried herself with. For three days, I stayed by her side, encouraging her to sit up and get out of bed. I bought fresh flowers to brighten up her room. It was such a small thing, but I knew it meant the world to her.

Yolanda, on the other hand, was conspicuously absent. She did a couple of things for show. A nurse stopped by one day and a caretaker the next. Since neither one of them knew where anything was, I knew they didn't stop by often. Two days turned into two weeks and the whole time I was there, not once did Yolanda come to check on her mother, say a few words, or even peek into the room. Her lack of concern was astonishing, but it also wasn't surprising, considering the recent history between us. She avoided my presence, yet the house remained full of her friends drinking and smoking as if a spectacle was being made of my mother's final moments. I later learned through my best friend who had been with me for moral support that Yolanda had made a horrendous comment to her: "Can she die already?" I couldn't fathom that kind of callousness coming from anyone, let alone her own daughter. It was horrifying.

Despite the constant tension, I did everything I could to create a sense of normalcy for my mother. I played her favorite gospel hymns, told her stories, and reminisced about happier times. I kept washing her hair, filing her nails, and tidying up around her, hoping to soothe her in some way. When she passed, the situation became even more complicated. Yolanda and I clashed over the arrangements. My mother had been a proud and active member of her church, serving on the pastor's supplement board and volunteering for years. I felt it was only right to honor her with a service there, where she belonged. That was her church home! But Yolanda wouldn't have it.

"No one at that old church cared about her," she argued dismissively.

I didn't care for her tone at all. *"At that old church."* The way she said it seemed to disregard the 30 years of mom's life she spent there honoring and serving the Lord. Her sole focus was cost. Her suggestion—something so casual and cold—was that we skip the service altogether, cremate her, and have a repast at Pappadeaux's. I was horrified.

"No," I said firmly. "Absolutely not. We're not doing that."

We reached a reluctant compromise: A wake with an open casket viewing and a funeral service, followed by cremation. I knew my mother's wishes were to be buried because she didn't believe in cremation, but there was nothing I could do. Yolanda still had all legal power. I went to the funeral home accompanied by my best friend, Sandy. She always came through for me when I needed her most. The director knew our family well and offered to embalm my mother's body at no cost, worried we'd regret not having that final moment to say goodbye. His generosity was a testament to how respected my mother was within the community. I took it as a small blessing amidst all the chaos.

I threw myself into planning the service. I called family members, coordinated with the church, and chose flowers and readings that my mother would have loved. I spent hours assembling a photo montage for the service. I reached out to Yolanda and mom's other daughter, Bebe, asking for photos. They both seemed disinterested, barely contributing to what should have been a collective effort. It hurt to realize how fractured things had become, especially with Bebe because I thought we were good.

When the day of the funeral finally came, I noticed Bebe's demeanor had shifted. She arrived separately, didn't join the family for prayers, and refused to speak to me. Her attitude was hostile and distant. During the video tribute, she abruptly stood up and stormed out, later claiming there were too many pictures of me and not enough of her. It was ridiculous, but I saw it for what it was—another symptom of the toxicity Yolanda had spread.

Yolanda and I kept our interactions civil during the service, but we were as cold and distant as the North Pole. I kept my focus on my mother, making sure I sent her home in a way that would have made her proud. I couldn't let petty grievances cloud the moment of farewell. After the service, we returned to the house for the repast. Bebe didn't show up. I remember standing there, looking around the room filled with people I hadn't seen in years and thinking, *"This is it. This is the last time I'll have to deal with Yolanda."* I left shortly after, taking only a few personal items back to Atlanta with me—a guest book and a couple of small mementos. It was all I could carry, emotionally and physically.

Despite the funeral being over, the legal battle with Yolanda was just beginning. I had already engaged an attorney to contest her handling of my mother's estate. I suspected she had forged signatures, changed life insurance policies, and siphoned off funds. It wasn't about the money. It was about ensuring that my mother's final wishes were respected and justice was served. The ashes became another point of contention. I had asked a friend to retrieve them from the funeral home, and they gave them to her in a simple bag. Then, I got a call. We needed to return the ashes because the bag wasn't in compliance. They were supposed to have been given to us in an urn. My friend brought them back, trying to do the right thing, only to be met with Yolanda's meddling once again. They never returned the ashes to me.

We went back and forth in court for what felt like an eternity. Yolanda flaked on agreements, fired her attorney, and pulled every trick in the book to delay proceedings. The only ones benefiting from all this mess were the lawyers. Eventually, we reached a settlement but Yolanda reneged on her promises and lost the house in the process. What little was left was split between her and Bebe. Everything else was gone: The family home, the heirlooms, the photos. All of it was lost in the mess of lies and legal wrangling.

I haven't spoken to Yolanda since. I doubt I ever will. The last time I saw her was in court, and even then, she felt like a stranger to me. The whole ordeal—the battle over my mother's estate, the funeral, the aftermath—changed me. It hardened me in ways I didn't think possible. It also taught me to stand up for what's right, no matter how painful, and to honor those who came before me, even when it feels like the world is trying to rewrite their story. My mother deserved better than what she got in the end, but I made sure her final journey was one of love and respect. In that, at least, I found a small measure of peace.

It's truly unfortunate how everything played out. Aunt Roz was the one person who did her best for me. She fought tirelessly to create a better life for me, taking on challenges that many wouldn't. At one point, she even placed me in a group home, not out of punishment but as a desperate measure to provide me with stability, resources, and support that I couldn't find elsewhere. She never gave up on me. In all of her efforts, I believe Mom simply wanted to ensure I was better equipped to overcome circumstances I didn't choose and to rise above the limitations of my past.

My mother wanted me to be more than just another success story. She wanted me

> *I believe Mom simply wanted to ensure I was better equipped to overcome circumstances I didn't choose and to rise above the limitations of my past.*

to thrive in a way she hadn't seen within our family, and she did her best to lay the necessary foundation. I can't imagine not fighting for her the way she fought for me. I think I channeled so much energy into ensuring her wishes were honored because I felt a deep obligation—a sense of guilt maybe—that I hadn't been more present in the last stages of her life. I often wonder what would have happened if I hadn't moved away to Atlanta. What if I'd stayed closer, been there for her in person when things started to deteriorate? Would it have changed anything?

Those questions haunt me, but I know my mother was proud of me. Still, that knowledge doesn't erase the pain of feeling like I missed the early signs of her needing me more. I think I got too fixated on building my life elsewhere and distanced myself from the cries for help that she sent out in her own quiet way. She was strong—maybe too strong—and it was only when it was too late that I realized just how long she'd been struggling alone.

It's taken me a long time to come to terms with the reality that her passing and everything that happened afterward were meant to be part of my journey. I believe her purpose in my life wasn't just to raise me but to instill in me the resilience and character to weather storms even after she was gone. I've come to see that she felt a deeper connection and responsibility toward me. Not because she didn't love her other daughters, but perhaps because I was her second chance—a chance to do things differently.

When I reflect on why I sought her guidance at such a young age and why I chose to live with her instead of my father, it all makes sense now. As a child, I was drawn to the strong women around me. My grandmother was that strength for me when I couldn't see it in my own mother. My father, God rest his soul, wasn't equipped to raise a young girl on his own. He did the best he could with his limited means, but he wasn't ready for the challenge of shaping me into the woman I am today. He had his own battles and shortcomings that prevented him from being the guiding hand I needed.

I think his absence, even though painful, was intentional. Had he stayed, he might have tried to keep me close in ways that wouldn't have been healthy for me. I needed the stability that Aunt Roz provided. I needed a home where I could see what hard work looked like, what it meant to be a woman of integrity, and experience the deep care she had for me. He even told me once that he'd called to check in on me many times but was blocked from interfering because Aunt Roz was determined to keep me grounded. Looking back, I understand now why she did that. She didn't want me to get caught in the cycle of instability, and it was the right call.

Being raised by her gave me a front-row seat to what success without compromise looked like. She showed me how to navigate through life with dignity and strength. At times, I wondered why she was so strict—why I couldn't wear makeup or go to certain places. Now, I see it clearly. She was preparing me, protecting me, and nurturing me in the ways that mattered most.

Mom taught me that I didn't need a man to define or complete me. That mindset has been a blessing and a curse. I saw her do it all alone and for the longest time, I thought I had to do the same. As I matured, I realized that it's okay to want a partner not out of necessity but out of a desire for companionship and support. It's a fine line between being fiercely independent and being open to receiving love and partnership. I'm still learning how to balance that, but I know she laid the groundwork for me to get it right.

Through everything, I wish she could have been here longer to see the person I've become, to see how her investment in me has paid off. I believe she did get it right with me. I didn't understand it all back then, but she set me on a path to become the woman I am today—a woman of purpose, strength, and resilience. It's only now that I see how intertwined my journey and hers were. She introduced me to church, to community, to the value of service, and to the significance of mental health. I started therapy at 12 and although I resisted it at first, I'm eternally grateful she pushed me in that direction. Therapy has been a consistent thread in my life, helping me confront the pain, the guilt, and the loss, but also guiding me toward healing.

Mom gave me a roadmap for navigating life's hardships with grace. She showed me the importance of self-care, not just in appearance but in every aspect of my life. She was the one who made sure I got my hair and nails done, who took me to the doctor, who taught me the importance of maintaining my health and well-being. I may have thought she was overbearing at times, but all those lessons have made me who I am today.

As I reflect on all that's happened, I understand now that everything—both the good and the bad—was designed to lead me to this point. Every painful experience has shaped me into someone who can use that pain to influence and inspire others. There's power in that, a power I'm still uncovering.

It's ironic that in losing Aunt Roz, I found a new strength within myself. It's the strength to keep going, to continue aligning myself with my purpose despite the setbacks. I know now that my purpose is to serve, to give back, to help others find their own strength and voice. Therapy has been a crucial part of that journey. My therapist once told me, "Choose purpose over pain." That simple phrase shifted everything for me. It reminded me that I don't have to be defined by what I've been through. Instead, I can use those experiences as stepping stones toward a greater purpose.

Prayer has also been my anchor. While I wouldn't say I'm overly religious, my connection to the spirit of God is strong. Losing so many loved ones has made me acutely aware of the angels I have watching over me. Their presence gives me peace and reassurance that I'm on the right path. What's helped me recover most though is love—being surrounded by good energy, by people who uplift and support me. I'm a firm believer that love heals. While some might say I have too many friends or too many people in my circle, I don't see it that way. I see it as surrounding myself with the energy that feeds my soul.

As I close this chapter of my life, I'm excited for what's to come. I'm excited to take all that I've learned and apply it to healthier relationships—with myself, my child, my partner, and my friends. I've learned that peace is love, and there is power in purpose.

Aunt Roz was my angel on earth, and now she's my angel above. Without her unconditional love and relentless effort, I'm not sure where I'd be today. But I do know this: I was always meant to be who I am. If it hadn't been her, it would have been someone else who would have stepped in and helped me find my way, but I'm so grateful it was her.

Through all the trials and tribulations, I now understand that my life has always been guided by a higher purpose. Every experience has led me to this point. As I continue on this journey, I'm more determined than ever to embrace that purposefully.

We all have the power to connect with our purpose and make sense of our pain. It's a journey of embracing, healing, and transforming. This second half of my life is dedicated to applying those lessons—to living with intention, to fostering healthier relationships, and to serving in ways that uplift others.

In the end, peace is love, and there is undeniable power in understanding your purpose. As long as I have breath in my body, I will continue to live out that purpose. For Aunt Roz. For myself. For everyone who needs to see that it's possible to rise above, no matter where you start.

Acknowledgments

$\mathcal{I}$ want to acknowledge my Angels who keep me covered and protected through this purpose journey:

DECEMBER 8, 1943–AUGUST 7, 1985

Queen, Queenie, Queen Esther Petty—I wish I got to know you! Many see that your spirit is living through me. I hear how you commanded a room, how beautiful you were, and how your energy was everything. Thanks for my cheekbones, legs, and inner beauty, Mom! I am me because you gave birth to your only baby girl.

APRIL 26, 1975–SEPTEMBER 6, 1996

Jock, Brother, Jarvis Hiriam Hargrove—Man, you were so cool. I always wanted to be around you and show you off to my friends. I watched you take care of so many at such an early age. You were a quiet giant that many looked up to. I am thankful for our time together; although it was short, some of my fondest memories are of you. I'm so glad to have a relationship with your children: Lorenzo, Jasmine, and Lalah. You would be proud! Often, my son reminds me of you, and I couldn't be happier about that. A piece of me is still missing on this earth, but I find healing in knowing you're protecting me daily.

MARCH 3, 1908-MAY 3, 2003

Grandma, Granny, Leatha Collins—I'm forever grateful for you being the first woman in power that I witnessed. You were respected for your business and took great care of your grandkids. It's because of you that I understand how important legacy is. You showed me that being a boss starts with taking care of your own so that you'll be in the position to take care of others. You are truly my foundation!

NOVEMBER 4TH 1950-FEBRUARY 5TH, 2017

Roz, Rozzie, Aunt Roz, Mother—Rosliard Marie Freeman—I always said you were my angel on Earth. What a woman to take in a little girl with zero questions asked. We were each other's second chance. Lady, I thank you for never giving up on me and for showing me how to navigate this world. Everything I have become is because you raised me to be confident, strong, uncompromising, and fierce. You were such a classy woman. Finding ways to love myself was not the easiest, but I now understand what you meant by your teachings, and I hear you. I owe this life to your work, and I will display your work throughout every step of this journey until my purpose is fulfilled!

OCTOBER 7, 1943-JULY 25TH, 2020

Jimmie, Smooth Jimmie, POP, PaPooh, Dad, Daddy, Uncle Jimmie—Jimmie Earl Hargrove—To know you is to love you. A gentle soul with a heart unlike any other. A gentleman who loved his only daughter. You made mistakes along the way, but you were such a great man. I never doubted your love; I just understood your capabilities. Our relationship was special, and I miss you so much. You started all of this, and I will finish it through. Thanks for your endless love, your spirit, and for giving me life.

QUEEN, ROZZIE, JARVIS, JIMMIE

To the living—my heartbeat, my only child, my Son, Tavaris Jalen Johnson—I am thankful that God saw fit for me to mother you. There is no greater blessing than the day you were born. You have taught me so much, and it's because of you that I continue to be victorious. I am in awe of you and so proud of the young man that you are. There is no greater accomplishment. Everything I do, I think about you and how I am a reflection of you and your legacy. You, son, are impressive, and I love you so much!

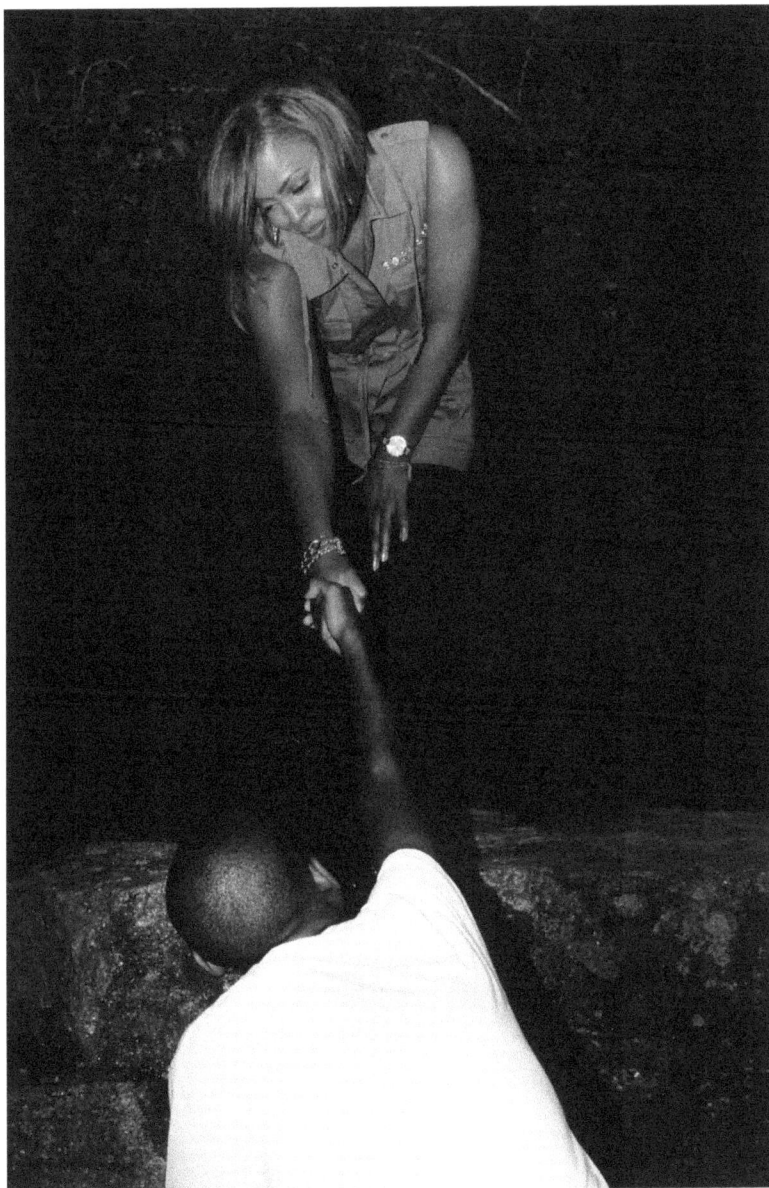

Milton Keynes UK
Ingram Content Group UK Ltd.
UKHW020051151124
451074UK00021B/194/J

9 781961 863934